# Be Rich Through Legacy Living

By Craig A. Anderson

Overflowing resources

Overflowing Resources Publishing Company
2620 S. Cleveland Avenue, Suite 205
St. Joseph, MI 49085

ISBN: 978-1-950012-03-9

United States of America

Overflowing Resources Publishing Company is a division of Family Focused Financial. www.famfocfinancial.com

Securities and Advisory Services offered through ***Harbour Investments, Inc.*** Member FINRA/SIPC.

*The examples in this book are for illustrative and educational purposes and are not intended to provide individual financial, tax, or legal advice. Every family situation is unique. Please consult a professional regarding your specific situation.*



Cover concept: Caleb Wilson
Cover design: Jennifer Cummings, using AI generated hourglass illustration, May 28, 2024.

Legacy Living / Craig A. Anderson—1st ed.

# Table of Contents

# Introduction

In this, the craziest story in the Generation Series, Lydia is crystal clear about wanting to retire and she is financially ready. However, she's missing some critical pieces in the puzzle to make her retirement really count. In *Legacy Living*, Lydia embarks on an adventure that provides meaning and purpose to retirement. Come, join her discovery…alone, or with a group.

This book includes a story to fuel your imagination, scriptures to recalibrate your perspective, and discussion questions to ignite your reflections and/or conversations. I hope you enjoy the journey!

# Credits

These amazing people gave helpful input starting from construction editing input to fine-tooth-comb-last-minute tweaks on the manuscript.

Thank you all for your thoughtful and careful feedback.

Hannah Lannigan (my dear daughter and writing coach)

Kathy Bradford (my dear sister and cheerleader)

Linda Diltz (a good friend and client)

Carol Brandt (a client who agree to proofread the manuscript between jobs)

Linda Diltz

Annabelle West (an employee with extra-strong English skills)

Linda Diltz (yes, she went through it three times)

Jennifer Cummings (an employee with creativity and unending patience)

# Section 1

# Waking Up

## *Must be Dreaming*

Lydia Barnes woke suddenly, her heart racing and her bed sheets soaked with sweat. Was it a hot flash, or was it that terrible dream she was having? While she slept, a burglar broke in and found her stash of cash under a drawer in the kitchen. The burglar thought no one was home, but she was sleeping in her bedroom, as usual. At least she *had* been sleeping, until a vase crashed to the floor. Then his clomping boots echoed down the hallway from the dining room. Her heart was pounding so hard she could feel it. She felt violated, scared, and angry that someone would break into her house. If only Rick was still alive, he would confront this burglar and protect Lydia. Rick had been gone for several months now, but she had not completely adjusted to her new reality.

Would she confront this burglar herself, or flee out the patio door of her bedroom? His footsteps were coming closer, and she could even hear his heavy breathing. Her breathing quickened. As she slipped out of bed and peeked from behind her bedroom door, she caught a glimpse of a gun in his hand. He turned into the room next to hers. Confrontation was no longer an option; she would have to sneak out the patio door or risk being shot. As she unlocked it and began to open the door, it squeaked. She froze, hoping he hadn't heard it. She wasn't sure if she was more angry or more scared. Fortunately, he was loud enough opening closet doors and dumping things on the floor, that he didn't hear her. She ducked into the night and ran next door to a trusted neighbor. But instead of it being her neighbor's house, it was her bank, and it was open.

She entered the bank in her pajamas, but no one seemed to notice or care what she was wearing. She asked to withdraw all her money so she could make sure it was safe. The teller tried to persuade her otherwise, and explained they had a special on pizza. This didn't seem any more unusual to the teller than the fact that she was wearing pajamas. She explained to the teller that she just wanted her money.

The teller had Lydia sign a form, then went to inform the branch manager. After a moment, she was ushered into the manager's office, where she sat waiting while the manager collected cash from the vault. He brought two grocery bags into his office. He handed her one of the bags and mentioned that it represented her share of the withdrawal she was making. That sounded strange for some reason, but she couldn't figure out why. She thanked the manager, and as she stepped outside, her favorite park, located several blocks away, was somehow across the street.

Lydia decided to go for a walk. The sun was out, and birds, squirrels, and people were all enjoying its warmth. It occurred to her that it was now the middle of the day, and she had become hungry, so she walked to a vendor where she occasionally bought lunch. The grocery bag was heavy, so she set it on the ground while she ordered her meal. When the vendor told her how much she owed, she leaned over and reached into her grocery bag to grab a $20 bill. She paid the vendor, but when she turned back, the man who had broken into her house was standing next to her. She froze. She couldn't even scream as he quietly picked up the bag and walked away. The vendor calmly handed her back her change as if nothing had happened. She felt horrified, devastated, and violated. What would she do next?

As she walked through the park, which had turned into a different park along the river, a hunched and haggard woman limped over to her, begging for money. She had a sweet smile on her face and held her hand out for a donation. Lydia explained that she had just been robbed and didn't have any money.

The woman inquired in a knowing tone, "Not even some change?" Lydia remembered the change the vendor had given her. This was all the money she had. She numbly handed it over. The woman looked her right in the eye with a playful grin, straightened up, and ran away. It had been a scam. These three people had taken almost all of her money.

Lydia began to chase the woman. She was catching up when the beggar woman suddenly crossed the sidewalk at the edge of the park and jumped into a car driven by the man who had robbed her. The bank manager was in the back seat holding up two grocery bags, presumably with all her cash. They drove off in celebratory and mocking laughter.

Lydia ran after them, yelling and crying and panting. She wanted to catch them, bring them to justice, and get her money back. Before she could decide what to do next, she woke up in a sweat with her heart racing. The sheets were drenched with her perspiration and her pillow moistened with her tears.

## Or Was It a Dream?

It had been a terrible dream. Her heart was still racing. She still felt angry and scared as the reality of the dream faded. But before she had completely calmed herself down, she sensed there was someone in the bedroom with her. Looking over at the window, she could see the silhouette of a man sitting in her reading chair. Her heart accelerated to an even faster pace than before. Was it Rick? No, he was dead. Maybe it wasn't a dream after all, and this was the burglar? Her heart was beating so fiercely she was afraid she might die of a heart attack. But she was so angry that she wanted to pick up the lamp beside her bed and throw it at the man. He might still shoot her, but at least she could hurt him before he took all her money.

However, before she picked up the lamp, he spoke. His voice wasn't gruff as she would have had expected. It was very gentle, even peaceful.

Visitor: Lydia, it was your time to leave, but you have been granted an extension.

Lydia: What are you talking about?

Visitor: While you were sleeping, a burglar came into your house. I sent him away and he will never return.

Lydia, *still in shock and not knowing whether to trust this man:* Who are you?

Visitor, *disregarding her question:* You have accumulated a little money, but you are poor toward God. You are being given another year to become rich.

Lydia, *objecting quickly:* What do you mean, "a little money"? Rick and I saved over three mil…

But he was gone. He didn't get up and leave, he was just gone. At least she thought he was gone. It was dim in the bedroom. Maybe he slipped away. She unplugged the weapon-lamp beside her bed and walked through the house carefully searching each room. The vase in the dining room was not broken after all. Everything was in order and her house cash was right where she kept it—hidden under the bottom cupboard drawer next to the refrigerator.

She wondered what had just happened. She had obviously had a terrible nightmare, but she was sure she was awake when the man spoke to her.

She checked her phone. It was almost 4 a.m. She laid back down in bed to get some more sleep. Her heart was still racing but her mind was racing even faster.

What just happened? Did she have a burglar in her house, or not? Was this second guy an angel? What did he mean by, "Lydia, it was your time to leave"? Was she going to die? Did he say she had another year? Only a year? Did that mean she was going to die in a year? She wasn't ready to die. What did he mean by, "poor toward God and rich toward God"? Were most of her liquid savings still in the bank?

It became clear that she was not going to get back to sleep, so she decided to get up. Completely distracted by her dream, she assumed it was a workday, and got ready as normal. Then she realized it was Saturday morning. But instead of changing again, she decided to go to the bank to check on her savings accounts just in case any of this had been true. She needed a sanity check.

She arrived and waited in line. Finally, her turn came, and she approached the next available teller, who in fact was the one who had been in her dream. After inquiring about her current balances and being assured how much she had in total, the branch manager approached her with a friendly greeting. He was also the manager in her dream. She was relieved that he hadn't run off with her cash after all.

He waved her back into his office. As she sat down in front of his desk, he commented that her largest CD had a month left, then squirmed a bit as he was looking for the right way to ask his next question. He finally just blurted it out.

Manager: I'm so sorry to hear the news. How long do you have…I mean, how long have they given you?

She didn't know how to answer him. This normally would have been an awkward question, but considering her dream, she had no idea how to take his question or how to answer it. Did he know what she had just encountered? Was he part of some scam after all? She looked confused.

Lydia *mumbling:* I don't know what's happening.

With no farewell, she stood up and walked out the door in a state of shock.

She needed to clear her mind and sort things out. Coming to the bank had not helped as she hoped it would. Maybe a walk would help. She took off at a leisurely pace and ended up several blocks away at her favorite park. Lydia saw the vendor who had been in her dream but wondered if she dared to approach him. Wanting reassurance that she wasn't crazy even more than she wanted to eat, she stepped up to the food wagon. The vendor told her with great jubilation that he was planning to retire in a year and leave. He explained that he would be moving south to enjoy warmer weather. Then he turned to her with an innocent question.

Vendor: How about you…how long before you leave?

She wondered why he was suggesting she would leave. That was the same word that the visitor used. Did everyone know something she didn't? What was going on?

Then she remembered discussing cold winters with this man previously and the possibility of moving south someday. Maybe this was all he was referring to. But he was leaving in a year…what a coincidence.

Lydia had no sooner left the food wagon when she received a call from her bank. The manager called and apologized profusely for mixing her up with someone else who was recently diagnosed with Lou Gehrig's disease. They both laughed with relief. Through an awkward chuckle, he recounted that she looked so confused when he had made inappropriate comments. Again, he apologized, told her he wouldn't keep her, and they said their goodbyes. Everything about his call made sense and should have provided some reassurance that this was all a mistake or misunderstanding. But when he said, "Goodbye," something about the word hit her as much as his original gaffe. There was a finality to it that he did not intend to convey, she was sure. But it came across to her, nonetheless.

As she hung up, a woman approached her who looked very similar to the one in her dream; haggard, bent over, limping. She would have walked away quickly if they had not already made eye contact. From the greasiness of her hair, it was obvious this woman had not showered in a while, and as she came closer, Lydia could see the grime on her clothes and was overpowered by the smell of urine and body odor.

But unlike the woman in her dream, this lady did not have her hand out. She seemed determined to reach Lydia, as if she had been trying to catch up to her. As Lydia began to explain she didn't have any money on her, the woman held up her hand as if to say, "That's not why I'm here."

Beggar woman, *through squinting eyes:* I heard a voice. That happens to me, you know?

Lydia thought to herself, "Not surprising." The woman waited, as if needing Lydia to agree with her before proceeding. After a long awkward pause, and realizing Lydia wasn't going to affirm anything, she continued.

Beggar woman: The voice said that you don't have much in your account, and that you only have a year to change it.

Then she cackled a loud laughing cough and wandered away, mumbling to herself.

Lydia, *out loud, but to herself:* That was weird, and I am definitely not dreaming right now.

Now she was confident that someone was trying to get her attention. Was it God? Did he really exist? If so, why would he send her any messages? She hadn't talked to him since she was a girl. What did this all mean? What was the point? What was she supposed to change?

## *Who to Tell?*

Lydia still wasn't sure how much of what she had experienced that morning was dream and how much was reality, but she had a sense that there was a distinct message that she shouldn't ignore.

The next week at work was very ordinary, with no bizarre dreams or conversations. There was, however, one special event. On Friday, there was a departmental meeting where the salesperson of the year was recognized. Lydia was awarded the title for that year; it had been her best year of sales ever. She was applauded by her colleagues for this achievement.

After the meeting, her boss took the whole sales department out to lunch. Lydia enjoyed the time out of the office, but she was surprised that she didn't feel happier or more satisfied. Was she distracted by the puzzle she was trying to solve, or was she sobered by the fact that she barely won the award?

Patty, the woman who earned the same award the last two years, had been on track to win again. No one had ever won three years in a row. However, Patty contracted an aggressive cancer and died several months ago. If Patty had not died, Lydia would not have won this award. It struck her, like a cold gust of air, how much could change in a year. That award had meant so much to Patty the previous year, and she seemed very pleased that she would likely earn it three years in a row. Lydia thought to herself, "What did it matter now? Not much," she concluded. She wondered if Patty had received the same kind of warning that Lydia had, if Patty would have done anything differently in her last year.

On the way home from work that afternoon, Lydia noticed a new "For Sale" sign in front of one of the houses on her block. It reminded her of the plan she and Rick had before he died to sell their house and buy a larger one. Lydia wanted a place that could house each of their children's young families in their own room when they came home for the holidays. When they were younger, they couldn't afford to do this, but they had worked hard and saved faithfully over the years and finally got to a financial position where they could make this change. Rick was okay with the idea because it would increase the value of their estate over time, but when he passed away, this plan went on hold. She had recently been wondering if she should restart this process, though it seemed overwhelming to think about going through all their stuff, packing, and moving all by herself.

Lydia and Rick could retire any time they chose, according to the financial advisor at their bank. She had so looked forward to taking life easy and pampering herself. After losing Rick, all that had evaporated. Again, she realized how quickly things can change. Her thoughts drifted back to the dream and the weird experiences of the previous Saturday. She still didn't know what to make of it all. It had faded, like memories do, although she knew it was real, and she knew it was for a reason. But who could she tell? Most people would think she was imagining the whole thing, or that she was reading too much into it. That's when an idea occurred to her.

What if she visited her cousin, Jackie Powers? Jackie lost her husband, Ron the year before Rick died, and at both funerals they had invited each other to "come for a visit." Jackie came to see her once, but Lydia was quite distracted during most of the visit. In the busyness of life, Lydia had not taken the time to go visit her. Lydia dealt with necessary details and thoughtlessly slid back into her normal routines as a method of coping with her sudden and deep loss.

She decided that Jackie would be the perfect person to confide in. She had always been a supportive person and a good listener. And she knew Jackie and Ron had been people of faith, so maybe she wouldn't think that her dream and experience was completely crazy. Maybe she could even help her solve the mysterious riddle.

## *On the Way to Jackie's House*

As she drove, she passed through one familiar town after another. Jackie and Lydia had grown up in the same town, so the journey to Jackie's house was like coming home. As she grew closer, her mind wandered to her childhood. She replayed many fond memories, like playing hide-and-go-seek or listening to vinyl albums on a turntable and singing along with their favorite songs. But then came *the* memory, like a worn-out record, of the night her father came home in a daze.

Ben Leitner was normally happy to see his children when he got home and would often pick them up and swing them around as they squealed in delight. But not on this night; *this* night he was more serious than she could ever remember. Her mother read his face and immediately left supper preparation to gently lead her father into their bedroom to talk. A while later, they emerged from the bedroom and gathered the children.

Ben: Kids, I have something to tell you. You know I planned to leave my business to you someday. *(He looked like he was fighting back tears.)* That is no longer possible.

The children chorused: Why not, Daddy? What happened? Why?

Ben: Our accountant has embezzled a very large amount of money from our company over the last several years. We owe our vendors so much money that we will have to sell our house, and it still won't be enough to repay all our debts.

He paused as something seemed caught in his throat.

Ben: The company is closing, and we will have to move. My attorney warned me not to put too much trust in one person, but I wouldn't listen, and now I must pay for my stubborn foolishness…*and* for another person's dishonesty.

Lydia didn't know what the word "embezzlement" meant, but she knew that, whatever had happened, it had shattered her father and ruined his company. She couldn't recall if her decision was immediate or gradual, but it became very clear to her that she never wanted to be in the same position as her father—vulnerable to the ethical decisions of others.

This commitment had influenced her choice of a marriage partner. Lydia wanted someone as dedicated to building wealth as she was. It also influenced her choice of work. She found a sales job where she could largely control her income and value to the company. It also ruled out using any investment vehicles that could lose money because of a drop in the market. This limited her choices to bank accounts, short-term treasury notes, and fixed annuities.

Lydia admitted to herself that she had probably missed out on some good growth in the market over the years, but she had never lost money in the market either. The tradeoff was worth it to her, even though her workmates did not understand her caution. In fact, they teased her for being overly conservative with her money. This didn't really bother her since she wasn't competing with them, like some of them seemed to be doing with each other. She was avoiding danger. Her childhood memory played over and over in her mind as if to reassure her she was on the right track.

Now, she looked back on a lifetime of hard work, frugal living, and consistent saving. But for the first time, she questioned if she had chosen the right path. Lydia didn't regret how careful she had been, but she wondered if she had missed something even more important along the way.

Her thoughts turned to Jackie in hopes that her cousin could provide some answers.

## *Safe at Home*

By the time Lydia pulled into Jackie's driveway, it was dusk. What a comforting sight to see the front porch light on. It said to her, "I am expecting you, you are at the right house, you made it safely, and you are welcome here." She had never noticed all those messages before and decided she would make it a point to turn her front light on when expecting company from now on.

Before Lydia had made her way to the front door, Jackie came out of the house to greet her with a strong, warm hug. They were such close friends as children, but Lydia had moved away. They saw each other at reunions, weddings, and funerals, but it was not the same as living a few blocks apart and sharing deep secrets during frequent sleepovers and phone calls. That didn't seem to matter now. Jackie hung onto her as if to say, "Welcome home, my dear cousin and friend."

Lydia didn't know why, but she started to tear up. Instead of pulling away from what could have been a cordial embrace, Jackie held her close, making a safe place for Lydia. The memories of their childhood flooded back in an instant. So did the memories of losing her husband and the memories of her dream a few weeks ago. Suddenly Lydia was pouring out tears—tears of happiness at seeing Jackie and tears of grief for what she had lost and for her fears about her future. Jackie just held on to her and cried with her.

When they finally let go and stepped back to look at each other, Lydia knew she had done the right thing to come here. Whether she got the answers she was looking for or not, she would be safe here. She could let her guard down, physically and emotionally, like she had not been able to do since Rick died. At the very least, she knew she would be allowed to continue grieving and healing from the horrible wound his leaving had caused.

Lydia's own children had been available and supportive after Rick's death, but they too were grieving, and she felt she needed to be there for them, to be strong for them. Therefore, she never let herself completely crash. This was different, however. She knew Jackie was here for her. And she wanted to be here for Jackie, in case the same was true for her.

Jackie: Can I get you something to eat?

Lydia: That would be great. I was so anxious to see you I didn't stop on the way.

Jackie, *smiling:* Well, let's go in and take care of that.

She hooked her arm in Lydia's and walked her inside.

# A New Day

The next morning, Lydia slept much later than normal. She had agreed to Jackie's offer *not* to use an alarm, but never dreamed she would sleep this late.

She could hear Jackie quietly clinking around in the kitchen and immediately felt guilty, like she should have been helping. She whisked her robe on and hurried down the stairs, as if late to a meeting.

Jackie, *coming to give her a good morning hug:* G'morning, Cuz. How long did you say you can stay?

Lydia, *regretfully:* A week, if that's okay.

Jackie: Of course.

Lydia: I have plenty of vacation time accrued, but there are some accounts that will need my attention by then, so I'll need to get back.

Jackie, *smiling:* I'll take what I can get and we'll make the most of it.

After filling their plates, they sat down to eat. Lydia almost forgot that Jackie and Ron always prayed before meals. Jackie started talking to God as if he had just joined them for breakfast. Lydia was envious that Jackie was so comfortable at this.

Jackie, *after swallowing her first bite of eggs and bacon:* You said you wanted to tell me about a dream.

Lydia, *buttering her toast:* Yes, but where do I start?

☙ ❧

The plates were long empty, and the coffee was at room temperature, but they still sat quietly after Lydia shared her story.

Jackie: I have a question.

Lydia: Okay?

Jackie: What difference would it make if you had one year to live or twenty years? I mean, how would you live differently if you knew you only had a year left?

Lydia: That's what I've been trying to figure out. I think I would have had a clear answer a month ago, before my dream. I would have spent more time visiting my kids and traveling. But what does "rich toward God" mean? I know that should be a part of my focus, but I don't know what it means. Do you know, Jackie?

Jackie: Hmm. I think I know, but I'm not sure how to explain it. While you're here, I want to introduce you to some people who are helping me understand it better. I volunteer a couple days a week. I was going to skip this week with you being here, but maybe we are supposed to go together.

# Section 2

# Living Today by Faith

## Hilarious Giving

As Jackie and Lydia walked through the back door of the soup kitchen, their first greeting came from Karla. It was a laugh and a hug at the same time. It wasn't that something funny had happened, but Karla's overflowing jar of laughter was easily tipped, and her chuckles just spilled out onto everyone in the room.

Her hair was tousled, and her worn jacket was oversized, but Lydia only noticed those details after she was already infected with Karla's contagious laughter.

Jackie: I've missed you, Karla, and your laughter.

This tipped Karla's jar again, and out splashed a new batch of giggles. But her jar didn't seem any emptier.

Jackie: I want you to meet my cousin, Lydia.

Karla, *laughing again and extending her hand:* Nice to meet you, Lydia.

Then, before Lydia could respond, Karla grew serious as she remembered the sandwich bag in her pocket, full of one- and five-dollar bills. She pulled the bag out carefully and handed it to Jackie.

Karla, *with a twinkle in her eye:* Here. Please add this to our fund.

Jackie: I still have the money from last week. Can you tell me what you are saving it for?

Karla, *surprised:* Saving it? I'm not saving it for anything. This is a giving fund.

Jackie, *equally surprised:* Oh, I thought you wanted me to save it for you.

Karla, *laughing heartily:* Goodness, no.

Jackie: I'm sorry. I misunderstood. I thought you were giving me money for safekeeping. I thought you were saving up for a down payment on rent, or something like that.

Karla, *her laughter resumed:* Oh, heaven's no. I stay in a basement apartment in my sister's house. She and her husband both have good-paying jobs, but not much time. I cook, clean, and do laundry for them, plus help them watch the kids…kind of like a nanny and a maid combined. They give me room and board and spending money. Win, win. *More laughter.*

Jackie, *her eyes misting:* Karla, I've only known you for a few months, but it seems like you are giving to people all the time. Why would you give me money to give away?

Karla, *spilling more chuckles:* Oh, I do love to give.

Then she turned to Lydia.

Karla, *still spraying giggles:* You know how money gives you pleasure?

Lydia, *hesitantly:* Yes.

Karla: I mean, it feels good to buy some new clothes.

Lydia, *even more hesitantly:* Yesss.

She wondered how long it had been since Karla had known *that* particular pleasure. Oddly enough, Lydia felt even more conspicuous about how smartly she was dressed than by how frumpy Karla looked. Lydia wondered if she would stand out as not belonging here this morning because she looked so professional.

Karla: But…when you give money to someone else, it feels even better than spending it on yourself. Right?

Jackie quickly agreed, and Lydia did not respond as she moved from distracted to confused.

Karla: And…the other person feels cared for…and they get the pleasure of spending the money on something they need.

Jackie: That's beautiful.

Karla: I figure, if giving ends up buying the same amount of stuff as spending, but brings pleasure to two people in the process, then the same amount of money is worth twice as much when we give it rather than when we spend it. *More chuckles.*

Jackie, *suddenly understanding:* Oh, that's genius, Karla! I never would have come up with that.

Karla: Well, a few weeks ago, I realized that if you double the value of your money by giving it away…then it must be worth three times as much if you give it to someone else to give away. *Laughing*, do you get my math?

Jackie: It makes so much sense when you put it that way.

Karla: Not only that, but if I give you money to give away, I can help people I don't even know.

Jackie, reaching out to hug Karla: Oh, Karla, I love your heart. I want to be like you when I grow up.

Karla spilled out more laughter and gave Jackie a deep hug in reply.

Just then, Bill came in the back door of the kitchen. He was of average height, but he was handsome, and somehow distinguished despite wearing jeans and a denim shirt.

Bill: Good morning, everyone!

He reached out to Karla to shake her hand, but she reached out her arms for a hug.

Karla, *hugging him and spraying laughter on his shoulder*: Come here.

Bill, *chuckling and returning the hug:* Good morning, Karla.

Karla, *giggling:* Mornin' Bill.

Bill, *turning to Jackie and shaking both hands.* Good morning, Jackie!

Jackie, *somewhat formally and with a slight blush:* Good morning, Bill.

Bill, turning to Lydia: And whom do I have the pleasure of meeting here?

Jackie, *interrupting her own thoughts:* Sorry, Bill. This is my cousin, Lydia.

Bill, *taking her hand in both of his and looking her in the eyes:* Hello, Lydia. Welcome.

Lydia, *overcome by his sincerity:* Nice to meet you.

It was like all these volunteers were coming to work, but Lydia thought that this felt nothing like going to her workplace. This wasn't just a job. She could tell these people really cared for each other.

Jackie, *shifting into a businesslike tone:* Well, Jennifer and Janice are not going to be here this morning, so it's just us.

Bill, *cheerfully:* Okay, what's on the menu?

Lydia: Scrambled eggs, sausage links, English muffins, and orange juice.

Karla, *laughing:* That's perfect.

Janice, *slipping through the door wearing scrubs, and saying in a quiet and friendly tone, but to no one in particular:* Good morning! Sorry I'm late…I just got off late shift.

Jackie, *surprised:* Good morning, Janice! How was your trip? I didn't think you were supposed to be back so soon.

Janice: We weren't. It was rainy most of the time, so we came back early.

Bill, *sympathetically:* Oh, that's too bad.

Janice, *dryly:* Right? Don't you feel sorry for me? We had rain on our vacation. *Then turning serious, she said,* No, it was one of the best things that could have happened. We were cooped up in our cabin in the mountains and we talked and talked and talked. We dealt with some pretty deep stuff. I don't think we would have done that if it wasn't for the rain.

Karla, *with a puzzled laugh:* Jerry talked?

Janice: I know, right? In fact, he talked most of the way home. Once he opened up, he *really* opened up.

Karla, *laughing:* I wish I could get my boyfriend, Roger, to talk like that. Maybe it's because I never stop. *Laughing some more.*

Janice, *noticing Lydia:* And who do we have here?

Jackie: Janice, this is my cousin, Lydia.

Karla laughed, knowing what was coming.

Janice, *taking Lydia's hand and kissing the back of it ever so gently:* Hi Lydia, you are loved.

Lydia, *laughing awkwardly:* Oh, really?

Janice, *looking Lydia in the eye:* I didn't get much love when I was a kid. I grew up, well, I didn't really grow up. I lived like a lot of the people you'll meet this morning…drugs…people coming and going…getting shuffled from one place to another…not feeling noticed, except when I was in the way…or when someone was abusing me. You know what I mean?

Lydia, *shrugging awkwardly:* Not really. I'm sorry.

Janice: Well, Jerry noticed me, and he even seemed to like me. *Laughing awkwardly and glancing at the clock,* I'm sorry I came in late, and now I'm making us even later by boring you with my story.

Lydia: It's not boring.

Janice: If you're interested, I can tell you more after breakfast, okay?

She started pulling last night's silverware out of the dishwasher.

Jackie assigned herself to the eggs, including both scrambling and serving them. She assigned Karla to warm and serve the sausage links, Bill served the English muffins, and Lydia was on orange juice duty. Janice put out the clean forks, trays, and glasses.

Since Lydia was last in line next to Bill, and they each had very little to prepare, it was natural for them to chit chat while they waited for the door to open.

Bill: How long are you here for, Lydia?

Lydia: Oh, I'm just visiting for a week. How long are you here for?

Bill, *his smile turning serious:* We never know, do we? It might be 15 years, or 15 minutes.

Janice, *overhearing his statement as she walked behind them:* Right?

Lydia, *trying to change the subject:* Bill, what do you do?

Bill, *trying to find an explanation:* Well, I…

Karla, *standing on the other side of Bill from Lydia, laughing again, but leaning behind him and whispering to Lydia:* He's loaded. He owns a bunch of businesses, but he never brags about it. He just gives most of his money away…he's rubbing off on me…except for having a lot of money. *Laughing boisterously.*

Lydia looked at Bill.

Bill: I am loaded…with blessings. God has been very good to me.

Lydia: What's your story? How'd you get there?

Bill, *thoughtfully:* Hmm, I grew up in a very poor family. We were in survival mode most of the time.

Lydia: I *can* relate to *that.*

Bill: Then shortly after us kids all moved out; my parents were both killed in a head-on collision by a drunk driver.

Lydia: Oh, I'm sorry to hear that.

Bill: Thank you. It was very hard at the time, but in the process, I learned some important lessons.

Lydia: How so?

Bill: We sold my parents' house and my siblings fought like alley cats over what little money was left. I didn't fight, so I didn't end up with much.

Lydia: I'm sorry.

Bill: That's when I decided if I was ever going to have anything, I couldn't depend on anyone else. I was going to have to get it for myself.

Lydia: That's so true. I agree with you.

Bill: It is true. But it's also empty.

Lydia: What do you mean?

Bill: It's kind of a long story.

Lydia: Well, it doesn't look like the door is open yet.

Bill: Okay. Well, I started my first business at age 16. I did window cleaning. Store owners from downtown needed their front windows cleaned and I got so fast, it was cheaper for them to hire me than to have their own employees do it. I really hustled. After a few years, I had built up a lot of business customers. One day, Mrs. Porter pulled me aside. She was one of my customers and had been watching me for some time. She said I had what it took to run her business. I objected because I didn't know anything about running a store, but she pointed out all the skills I already had and said she could teach me the rest.

Lydia: What did you do?

Bill: I was just going to quit, but Mrs. Porter suggested I train someone to wash windows and keep that business running while I started working for her.

Lydia: Wow, that's smart!

Bill: Don't get me wrong, she didn't make it easy. She made me work hard, learn every aspect of the business, even the ones I couldn't care less about.

Lydia: How did that turn out?

Bill, *sadly:* A few years later, she passed away.

Lydia: I'm sorry.

Bill: Thank you.

By that time, I had saved some money like she had taught me but didn't feel like I was making much progress.

Lydia: Did you find a better job?

Bill: Well, that's the thing. She had taught me how to run a business. It kind of gets in your blood, and I couldn't really see myself working for someone else at that point.

Lydia: So, what did you do?

Bill: It's what *she* did that changed the trajectory of my life. She left me her business.

Lydia: Really?

Bill: Yep. She had two kids she left money to, but neither one had any interest in her business, ever. She left it to me, including a business account with some cash, and instructions to train other people to help run my store and to buy the business next door.

Lydia: Wow, she was setting you up for success, wasn't she?

Bill: Exactly! The owner of the business next door was also getting on in years, and she wanted me to approach him about buying his business.

Lydia: And?

Bill: Come to find out, he had been holding on for me to buy his business. He and Mrs. Porter had already talked about it.

Lydia: Wow, she was *really* looking out for you.

Bill: I had no idea she was setting all this up for me.

Lydia: So, you own three businesses?

Bill, *bashfully:* Well, at one point I owned fifteen different businesses, plus some real estate.

Karla, *leaning over again and laughing:* He means a *lot* of real estate.

Bill, *smiling:* Now I'm down to my favorite five businesses and eight best properties.

Lydia, *teasing:* How does it feel to be rich?

Bill, *his expression turning serious:* Oh, money doesn't make you rich.

Lydia: What do you mean by that?

Bill: How much money does the average person want?

Lydia: I don't know.

Bill, *with a twinkle in his eye:* A little more.

Lydia, *chuckling:* I guess that's true.

Bill: It doesn't matter how much money you have. You never feel like it's enough. You always think of other people as being rich but not yourself.

Lydia, *more seriously*: That is so true.

Bill: Not only can money never make us *feel* rich because we always want more, but it can't actually *make* us rich either.

Lydia: I don't get it. If money doesn't make you rich, what does?

Bill: I had an uncle who watched what had happened between my siblings and me, and he noticed several years later how our lives were going. I think he was just trying to encourage me at the time, but what he said changed my entire outlook on money and life.

Lydia: What did he say?

Bill: He said, "Billy, did you know I'm a multi-millionaire?" Of course, he and my dad came from the same family. I told him, "I had no idea you had so much money." With a twinkle in his eye he said, "I have a beautiful wife, good kids, and my health, but I wouldn't trade any of them for a million dollars. I guess that makes me a multi-millionaire." Then he laughed, but it wasn't just because he was making a joke, it was a laugh of contentment. It hit me like a ton of bricks.

Lydia, *slowly and soberly:* It's kind of hitting me, too.

Bill: I had several businesses by then, and I was wearing myself thin to get more and more. It made me stop and think about what was really important. Shortly after that I met my wife. *That's* when I became rich.

Lydia looked at Bill for a long time.

Lydia, *slowly:* Thank you for telling me that.

Bill: Kind of makes you think, doesn't it?

Lydia: You have no idea.

Bill: It looks like we have our first customer. Good morning, Sherry!

# A.S.K. Principle

One of the last customers to come through the line was a man with short legs and a long beard. His clothes were well-worn, but clean.

Bill: Good morning, Phil!

Phil: Mornin' Bill! Man, it's crazy what's been happenin'. You're right about this askin' thing. I start askin' God for money and next thing I know someone offers me a job. Then I ask for a place to stay, and my sister asks me to house-sit while her family's gone on vacation. Dude, you almost got me believin' again.

Bill: That's great, Phil.

Phil: What's the rest of that thing you say?

Bill: A.S.K. Ask. Seek. Knock. Jesus said, "Ask and it will be given to you; seek and you will find; knock and the door will be opened to you. For everyone who asks receives; the one who seeks finds; and to the one who knocks, the door will be opened."

Phil: That's crazy, man. I never thought God would listen to a regular guy like me. I try to be a good person, but I'm not really. You know what I mean?

Bill: Yes, I do. God doesn't always give us exactly what we ask for, kind of like kids begging for candy right before supper. And he doesn't always answer right away. But he hears you, Phil, because he cares about you.

Phil: You're blowin' my mind, man. Crazy!

# *Richly Protected*

As they finished cleaning the kitchen, all the volunteers left one by one. Noticing Jackie was in the office doing some paperwork, and Janice was still tidying up, Lydia resumed her previous conversation with Janice.

Lydia: Janice, you said you grew up like a lot of our customers this morning.

Janice, *startled:* Yes. My dad had a steady job, and my mom worked on and off for cash. But my mom did drugs and my dad went to a local bar to drink away a good chunk of his paycheck every two weeks. So, we felt very poor.

When I was in high school, I would go down to the bar to drive my dad home. Jerry did the same thing for his dad. Of course, dad wasn't ready to leave until it was his idea. So, while we waited, Jerry and I would talk in the alley behind the bar. Well, I would talk, and Jerry would listen.

One night, I was alone, waiting in the alley. A drunk guy came out the back door like he was looking for me. He had been watching me for a while…real creepy, right? Anyway, I guess he thought he had a chance to make his move. I didn't know what to do. The alley ended behind some other stores, so there was only one way in and out. I might've been able to outrun him, but he had my escape route blocked. If I ran inside the bar, I thought my dad would be mad at me. This guy was plastered, but he looked big and strong. I just froze. I tried screaming, but only a squeak came out. He kept stumbling closer. I prayed for God to save me. I never prayed before that; it just came out.

I was imagining the worst and near a total panic when Jerry walked around the corner. He ran over to the guy, grabbed his shoulders, turned him around, looked him square in the eye, and pointed. The guy jerked away from Jerry's grasp and cussed at him, but he did finally leave. Jerry didn't say a word. I ran over to hug Jerry, and he just held me while I cried. Still, he never said a word.

After I stopped sobbing and sniffling, I didn't want to pull away from Jerry. I realized for the first time in my life, I felt safe. Jerry didn't let me go either. He wasn't trapping me, just protecting me. It didn't feel creepy or awkward. It just felt like I was where I belonged.

Jerry couldn't say what he was thinking, but he had tears in his eyes, and I wondered if this was more than a rescue to him. I hoped it was, but I didn't know...until the next week when he showed up at my house. When I came to the door, he just motioned with his head to say, "Let's go." I didn't need to ask my parents; *they* didn't care. And I didn't know where he was taking me; *I* didn't care. I just wanted to be with him, and evidently, he wanted to be with me, too. We went to a park where it was peaceful, quiet, and safe.

We started hanging out more. After graduation, we got married. I could talk to Jerry about anything. He always listened, but he never said much, especially about his feelings.

Boy, did that change on our vacation. I've asked him about his childhood before, but he never wanted to talk about it. This time it was different. He talked about how his dad would beat him and his mom when he was drunk. He told me how when he got older, he stood up to his dad one time and the beating stopped for a while. Jerry was bigger than his dad by then. But after Jerry moved out, his dad started beating his mom again. I started asking questions about how he felt toward his mom and dad and siblings, and he started talking and talking and talking. I think I learned more about what was going on in his family and inside his head than in all the years we've been together. I've trusted Jerry ever since that night in the alley, right? Now it's like he finally trusts me enough to let me in.

Lydia: Wow.

Janice: I know, right? A few years ago, I was working with a lady named Sofia. She's Jackie's niece. Maybe you know her?

Lydia: That name is not familiar to me. Is she on Ron's side of the family?

Janice: Oh, you're right, she's Ron's niece. Anyway, she and her husband, Roberto, had us over to their house for dinner and treated us like family. Then, we started getting together every week. They've taught us so much. Jerry and I both knew what we did *not* want in a family, but we didn't know *how* to have a *healthy* family. Sofia and Roberto have given us a picture of what a family could be. It's been amazing.

They've taught us how to set up a budget and save for a down payment on a house. They taught us how to fight fairly, instead of bullying or pouting or whatever.

But the one thing that blows my mind is how much they love us. And they would tell us so. I never heard that growing up. At first, I was suspicious, but over time they have helped us in so many practical ways, and they keep telling us how important we are to them and to God. They keep showing us and telling us how much we are loved. It has been a total revolution for me.

Lydia: That's amazing.

Janice: They invited us to go to church with them, and we weren't very interested at first. But we wanted to spend time with them, so we went along. Now we are learning things we never heard before. Most people don't escape the cycle of bad habits that we both grew up with, but between Sofia's family, God, reading the Bible, and the people at church, we are being rescued from repeating most of those same cycles. They have completely changed the course of our lives.

Now I know I'm loved, and I try to let everyone I meet know this, too. There are so many hurting people, and it's exciting to see them blossom when they realize how much God loves them.

Lydia, *with tears in her eyes:* Janice, thank you so much for telling me your story. You've given me hope that I could possibly be loved, too. My husband was always polite to me, but not so much with romance. We were two survivors working on the same team—side-by-side.

Janice reached out and gave her a gentle hug, and they cried together.

Janice: I understand. Jerry doesn't exactly overdo his affection either. Letting go, they laughed through tears and wiped away their mascara, which was running.

Janice, *adding seriously:* Lydia, God sees you and loves you. He wants a personal relationship with us so much that he is constantly trying to send us messages. But we aren't always listening, so sometimes he must turn up the volume to get our attention.

Lydia: Well, he's been turning up the volume on me lately.

All the way home, Lydia mentally played back the conversations she had at the shelter. God was clearly trying to get a message through to her, but what she was supposed to do about it wasn't as clear.

# What About Bill?

Jackie unlocked the front door before she and Lydia walked into the living room and instinctively dropped onto the couch, playing a duet of sighs.

Lydia: Tell me about Bill.

Jackie: Isn't he nice?

Lydia: And?

Jackie: And what?

Lydia: You see how he looks at you.

Jackie: What do you mean?

Lydia: Do you remember Nick Morrison?

Jackie: From high school? The one with a mullet who always wore a denim jacket?

Lydia: That's the one.

Jackie: What about him?

Lydia: You noticed how he kept looking at me before I did.

Jackie: He sure did.

Lydia: A little while later, he asked me out on a date.

Jackie: That's right.

Lydia: Well, that's how Bill looks at you.

Jackie: Nooo.

Lydia: Yesss. He's going to ask you out.

Jackie: No…Well, he kind of already did ask me out, but I think it's just…it's different.

Lydia: You don't like Bill?

Jackie: I didn't say that.

Lydia: You aren't ready to date anyone yet?

Jackie: I don't know.

Lydia: You want me to stop asking you questions?

Jackie: No, I'm okay talking about it.

Lydia: What do you think of him?

Jackie: I really like Bill. There have been a few guys showing special attention to me since Ron died, but he's one of the only guys I trust and admire enough to take seriously.

Lydia: So?

Jackie: I don't know. Ron told me he wanted me to remarry, so I don't feel like I would be unfaithful to him. But we had such a good marriage that I don't know if I could be happy with anyone else.

Lydia: Hmm.

Jackie: But I do get lonely sometimes. I want someone to listen to me, hold me, and tell me that's it's going to be okay.

Lydia: I hear that.

Jackie: And…someone to work alongside me and travel with me.

Lydia: Travel?

Jackie: Yes, Ron worked hard, but he didn't like to travel very much, so we stayed home most of the time. Even when he took time off for a "vacation" it was hard for him to leave. What if someone called to see a house and he wasn't here to show it? Or what if he had some big house project he wanted to finish? Vacation time was when he would work on those kinds of things.

Lydia: Not really a vacation.

Jackie: No.

Lydia: Yeah, Rick never wanted to spend the money, so we didn't travel very much either. We mostly took vacation pay and just saved it, along with every other penny we were hoarding.

Does Bill like to travel?

Jackie: Yes, but his wife had Lou Gehrig's Disease, and they couldn't travel toward the end.

Lydia: I already know he's handsome. Do you think so?

Jackie: Different than Ron, but yes, he is very distinguished looking. Quite handsome, really.

Lydia: How easy is it for you to talk?

Jackie: I don't know. I've kind of been avoiding Bill. I like so much about him that maybe I'm afraid I would fall in love with him.

Lydia: And that would be a problem because…?

Jackie: I don't know. My heart got ripped in half when Ron died. I don't know if I could go through that again.

Lydia: I'm sorry. It's been hard to let go of Rick even though we weren't as close as you and Ron.

Jackie: Really?

Lydia: Yes, really. We almost had a business relationship. Rick was so focused on making and saving money, and he was more of a brainiac than a feeler. Don't get me wrong, we hardly ever fought, but there wasn't a whole lot of passion either.

Jackie: Oh, I'm sorry.

Lydia: It's fine. We got along okay. It's just that…

Jackie: What?

Lydia: Well, sometimes when we would see a couple being romantic in public, Rick would be turned off and I would think, "Why don't you take some notes, Rick?" I mean, food tastes better with a little spice.

They both laughed, then paused for quiet reflection.

Jackie, *breaking the silence:* Plus, Ron was a great lover. I'm afraid I would be disappointed with anyone else. And how would it affect my kids and grandkids if I remarried?

Lydia: Those are important things to think about.

Jackie: But I *am* lonely. I enjoy spending time with God in the morning, and volunteering fills some of the emptiness, but I still come home to a quiet house every night.

Lydia, *looking around the room:* That's for sure.

What do you have to lose by letting down your guard a little with Bill…give him a chance to see where it goes?

Jackie *(Pausing and sighing):* You're probably right. I'm just not sure I'm ready.

Lydia: That's okay. You'll know when the time is right.

# Section 3

# Looking Ahead in Hope

## *Dying is the Best Place to Start*

The next morning, as Jackie and Lydia walked down the hall of the graduated care facility, they smelled a combination of disinfectant and body odor. They knocked on a door and heard a voice say, "Come in."

Jackie, *opening the door and walking into a sunny room:* Good morning, Jackson!

She walked over to where he was seated and leaned over to kiss his forehead.

Jackson, *his ivory teeth shining in between his ebony skin, and his rich, deep voice almost singing:* Mornin' Miss Jackie.

Jackie: This is my cousin, Lydia. She is here for a visit.

Jackson, *presenting the same smile and holding out his hand:* It's an hono' to meet ya', Miss Lydia.

Lydia, *taking his hand and shaking it:* It's nice to meet you, Mr…uh…

Jackson: Jackson.

Lydia: Nice to meet you, Mr. Jackson.

Jackson, *laughing:* No, ma'am…it' jus' Jackson.

Lydia: Oh, okay. Good morning, Jackson.

Jackie, *turning to Lydia*: Jackson is in hospice.

Jackson, *quickly, as if finishing a sentence:* She means I'm fixin' to die.

Lydia, *stunned by the abrupt and sobering report:* Oh, I am so sorry to hear that.

Jackson, *laughing gently:* Why be sorry? Is ya' s'prised dat someone's dying?

Lydia, *flustered:* Well...yes...I mean...no. Well, you seem quite matter-of-fact about it. Doesn't it trouble you?

Jackson: No ma'am. Ya' know anyone dat's *not* dyin', I mean, anyone dat's not gonna die someday? *He laughs again.* Ya' know, soon's we come out o' de hatch, we all slippery, and we sliding downhill all de way t' de grave.

He laughs again.

Lydia, *after a puzzled and awkward pause:* When you put it that way...

Jackson: Mos' people roll along as if it's neve' gonna happen to 'em.

Lydia: Probably.

Jackson: Oh, dying is de best place to start, Miss Lydia! When ya' think ya' got all kinds o' time, ya' jus' try to make ya'self comf'able. But when ya' know dey's only certain days lef', you try an' make 'em count, make a difference. Ya know what I mean?

Lydia did not respond.

Jackson: Miss Lydia?

Lydia, *returning from her distracted thoughts:* I'm sorry. Yes, I guess I've been one of the people you're talking about, just trying to make myself comfortable.

Jackson: Dat's right. Jus' natural. But when ya' funeral starts to comin' up on ya' real close-like, ya' start thinkin' to ya'self, "What kinds of nice things does I hope people gonna say 'bout me?" Den ya' start to wonderin' if dat's what they actually gonna say, or not. Den, ya' start thinking, "what I hab to do differ'ntly fo' people to say dose nice tings, and really mean it?" Dat all makes sense?

Lydia: I've never thought about it like that before, but it makes sense now.

Lydia felt as she had just found a new and dear friend, like she could talk about anything with this man. Before she knew it, she was telling him about her dream and the experiences in the bank and the park. He listened with a patient smile, his eyes growing brighter as she went. After her story she asked him one simple question.

Lydia: What do you think of that? Do you think I'm crazy?

Jackson: Miss Lydia, ya' been given a gif' like me, 'cept yours is jus' a little bigger'n mine, I s'pose. I don't have quite as long to live as ya', but at leas' we both know dat. It's like gettin' a second chance to undo some things an' do 'em up right. Ya know what I mean?

She marveled that he carried such gratitude instead of self-pity.

Lydia, *after a long stare of wonder and admiration:* Jackson, you are an amazing man. I am so glad Jackie introduced us. I needed to hear your words.

Jackson, *through glowing teeth:* See dere, Miss Lydia, ya' jus' made my day.

Lydia: How did you get this kind of perspective on life?

Jackson: I neve' went to college, but when I's in high school, de teacher would say, "Remember dis, it'll be on de final exam." I would pay special 'tention to dose tings.

Nows I don't read real good. But every day I spend some time in de Holy Bible o' God. I want to know what's on de final exam. Ya' know what I mean?

Lydia: No, I don't.

Jackson: Well, the Good Book, it say we all gonna' pass someday, den we hab to give an account o' ourselves to God. I see dat as de final exam.

Jackie: Jackson, I never thought of it that way.

Jackson: I'm getting' real close to the end o' my semester and the final's comin' up. I don' wanna flunk dat one, no ma'am.

Jackie: What do you think will be on the final exam?

Jackson: Dat's a good question, a real good question. Jesus, he say, no one comes to de Father 'cept by me. Ya' know what that means, Miss Lydia?

Lydia: When I was little, the pastor would say that Jesus is the only way to be rescued from sin and death and hell and the devil. Is that what you mean?

Jackson: Yes'm. He broke de power ob all dat evil when he died on the cross for our sins. Den' when we turn 'way from all dat evil and trus' him and follow him, he saves us. Dat's how we comes into his kingdom. But den dey comes a time, afta' we pass on, when we stand befo' the Almighty hisself and give account fo' ourselves. That's the final exam I's talkin' 'bout.

(Picking up his Bible) Let me read ya' somedin' I read jus' yest'day. Here it is, Luke 12:19-21, "And I'll say to myself, 'Yo' hab plenty a grain laid up fo' many years. Take life easy; eat, drink and be merry.' But God said to him, 'Yo' fool! Dis very night yo' life will be demanded from yo'. Den' who'll get what yo' prepared for yo'self? Dis is how it'll be with whoebber stores up things for deyselves but is not *rich toward God.*'"

Lydia, *perking up:* Where is that?

Jackson: Come outa' Dr. Luke's version of Jesus' story. Chapta' 12. Ya' neve' read it befo'?

Lydia: I heard that last phrase from my visitor, but like I said, I don't know what it means.

Jackson: Any ideas?

Lydia: No. If God made everything, he must be the richest person in the universe. How could we ever be rich compared to him?

Jackson, *chuckling lightly:* But ya' see Miss Lydia. It ain't *compared* to him…it's *toward* him *(as if that explained everything clearly).*

Lydia: But what does that mean?

Jackson: I reckon it means we makin' deposits in his bank so when we get dere, we's all set up.

Lydia: What do you mean by "deposits"?

Jackson: Can I reads you 'nother passage?

Lydia: Of course.

Jackson: Mr. Tim'thy, ya' see, he was taught by Mr. Paul hisself. He say…*(flipping pages)*…where's it at? Here it is. First Tim'thy, chapta' 6, startin' in verse sev'teen. "Command dose who rich in dis present world not to be arrogant no' to put dey hope in wealth, which is so uncertain,"…Dat's a fact…"but to put dey's hope in God, who richly provides us wid' ebrything for our 'joyment"…Oh that's good.

"Command dem do good, to b' rich in good deeds, and b' gen'rous an' willin' t' share." Now here's de bes' part. "In dis way they'll layup treasure for deyselves as a firm foundation for the comin' age, so'at dey may take hold ob the life dat is truly life."

What ya' think 'bout dat, Miss Lydia?

Lydia: Can I read that again?

Jackson *(handing her his well-worn Bible):* Most sure' can.

Lydia *(reading slowly, then looking up):* I haven't been a very good student, Jackson, but now that the final exam's coming up, and I need to get more serious.

Jackson: Dat's right. Ya' see, ma'am? Dis life jus' dress rehearsal…gettin' ready for da real thing. We can't eben imagine all the good tings he has waitin' fo' us. Dat's what I'm countin' on. Yes, ma'am.

Lydia, *introspectively:* Rich toward God.

Jackson: Yes'm.

Lydia: Good deeds and generosity?

Jackson: Yes'm.

Lydia: I don't know how to thank you.

Jackson: Ya' been a blessin' to me, Miss Lydia, that's fo' sho'. No need fo' thanks.

# *Where is Your Treasure?*

As Jackie and Lydia moved down the hall to the next room, Lydia was thinking about how much peace Jackson had at the thought of dying. She, on the other hand, was terrified. What if the visitor was right and she only had another year to live? She was *definitely* not ready.

Jackie, *after the door was unlocked and they were waved inside:* Good morning, Dorothy!

Dorothy was a short woman with almost-white hair, her nose almost sharpened to a point, and squinting eyes on the watch for anything suspicious.

Dorothy, *with abrupt determination:* You can't have any!

Jackie: Any what, Dorothy?

Dorothy, *her jaw tight like purse strings:* Any of my money. I know why you're here. You want my money, but you can't have it. I've hidden it where no one will find it. And that settles it.

Jackie, *changing the subject:* How are you feeling today, Dorothy?

Dorothy: Oh, I slept terribly. My arthritis keeps getting worse, you know.

Ever since I stopped giving my kids gifts, they've stopped coming to visit. I figured that was the only reason they came. Now I know for sure.

Jackie, *after listening patiently and sympathetically:* I'm sorry to hear that.

*Then, brightening after a pause:* Dorothy, there is someone I'd like you to meet. This is my cousin, Lydia.

Dorothy, *looking down:* What do you want?

Lydia, *taken back, but following Jackie's lead:* It's nice to meet you, Dorothy. I don't need anything.

Dorothy: Why is it nice to meet me? I'm not going to give you anything.

Lydia, *still flustered, but trying to recover:* Why would that matter?

Dorothy, *looking Lydia in the eye for the first time and lecturing sternly:* Because everyone wants something! If they don't get it, they move on.

*Then Dorothy pointed a crooked index finger at Lydia for emphasis.*

That's the key. Don't give it to them and they will leave you alone. And that settles it.

Lydia, *taken aback:* Oh!

Dorothy: I used to have friends, you know, lots of them. But I figured out they all wanted things from me, every one of them. I just wouldn't give them what they wanted, and sure enough, they eventually went away.

Dorothy, *after a pause:* except for this one here, *motioning to Jackie.* I still haven't figured out what she wants. She won't come out and ask, like my kids.

Jackie and Lydia exchanged a sad smile.

Jackie: Actually, Dorothy, there is something I want.

Dorothy, *turning her head away with disappointment:* See, I knew it!

Jackie: I want to know if there's anything you need, anything I can get you from the store, or anything I can do for you.

Dorothy: How much will you want me to pay you?

Jackie: Nothing, Dorothy, just let me do something nice for you.

Dorothy, *quizzically and skeptically:* You don't want anything from me?

Jackie: Nope. I just want to be friends.

Dorothy, *wiping a tear from her eye:* I'll think about it. *Then stiffening:* I'm sure you have other people to see. You should get along then.

She turned to walk into her bathroom.

Jackie: Goodbye, Dorothy. I'll see you next week.

There was no response except the sound of Dorothy blowing her nose.

As they left the room, Lydia couldn't help but think how much her own heart was like Dorothy's. Maybe she didn't speak as harshly as Dorothy, but she had a similar posture toward money. She couldn't help but compare Jackson's light heart with Dorothy's dark heart.

As they neared the next room, they heard music playing loudly, and someone was singing near the same key, even more loudly.

Eliza heard the knock and told them, "Come in."

As soon as they entered, she turned the music down, but not off, and she walked briskly over to Jackie to wrap her in a bear hug. She cupped Jackie's face with her plump hands, then hugged Jackie's hands with her own.

Eliza, *warmly:* Oh Jackie, how I've missed you…your beautiful smile and warm hands. How are you doing, dear?

Jackie: I'm doing well. Thank you, Eliza. There is someone I'd like you to meet. This is my dear cousin, Lydia.

Eliza, *embracing her hands instead of shaking them:* Oh, Lydia, so nice to meet you.

Lydia, *in mild surprise and sincerity:* The pleasure is mine.

Eliza: That's not *all* that's yours. I crocheted this doily for you.

Lydia, *in disbelief:* For me?

Eliza: Well, I didn't know it would be for you when I made it. I was talking to the Lord a couple mornings ago, and He told me to make it…said I would need it. Now I know who it was for.

Lydia, *still surprised:* But we've just met. You don't even know me.

Eliza, *pointing up:* Oh, Lydia. This meeting has been scheduled for a long time.

Lydia: What do you mean?

Eliza: Do you think the Lord, who made everything, is surprised that we are meeting today? *Not waiting for an answer:* No, Missy. He knows about every meeting, every word that is spoken, every thought that crosses our minds. He sees you, Lydia. He knows you…everything about you.

Lydia, *tearing up:* You really believe that don't you?

Eliza: Don't you? He even watches us when we sleep.

Lydia, *taken aback:* Oh, maybe he does. I went to church occasionally when I was little, but when my father lost his business…I guess we all kind of lost our faith, too.

Eliza, *sincerely:* I'm sorry to hear about your father's business. And I'm truly sorry to hear about your faith. *There was a long pause.* Maybe it'll come back and find you one of these days.

Lydia: I think it's trying to.

Eliza, *giving Lydia a thought break:* Jackie, how are you really doing? You don't have to be polite. You can be honest.

Jackie, *smiling and considering how to answer:* I'm very lonely, especially in the evenings.

Eliza, *reaching out for another hug:* Aren't they the worst? I'm sorry, dear.

As they pulled away, Eliza darted over to the kitchenette counter.

Eliza, *holding a plate toward Jackie with a homemade chocolate bar:* I have something for you, too.

Jackie, *with mock surprise:* Oh Eliza, you shouldn't have.

Eliza: Why not? Don't you like these anymore?

Jackie, *to Lydia:* Eliza's homemade chocolate bars are my greatest weakness.

It struck Lydia, as they were leaving, how Dorothy could have been a very beautiful woman if not for her suspiciously sour looks. On the other hand, Eliza wasn't very striking, but her gorgeous generosity made her attractive. She couldn't help but be drawn to Eliza's heart. Then she wondered about herself. What did she look like to others, and how did God see her heart?

She presumed an answer and decided she needed to change. When she got home, she would learn how to invest her time and money in other people, like Eliza.

## Assigning Where Things Go

Sherry, *hearing the knock:* Who's there?

Jackie: It's Jackie Powers.

Sherry, *slowly unlocking the door, and peering out to look both ways down the hallway before opening the door all the way:* Okay, come in.

*As soon as they were inside, she locked the door behind them.*

Jackie: Good morning, Sherry.

Sherry, *wiping the doorknob with two antiseptic wipes, then explaining:* You can never be too careful.

Jackie: I'd like you to meet my cousin, Lydia.

Sherry, *nodding her head cordially:* Hi, Lydia.

Jackie: What have you been up to since I saw you last week?

Sherry: I've been reviewing my will.

Jackie, *sarcastically:* Sounds like fun.

Sherry: I have it all mapped out, who's getting what.

Jackie: Ron was good about that. We had everything set up.

Sherry: It should be smooth sailing for my kids. I have my power of attorney in place in case I am disabled in some way. And I have a trust that divides up everything according to plan. And then there's a pour-over-will, just in case I forgot anything. It pours any leftovers into the trust.

She got up to straighten a picture that didn't look crooked to Lydia.

Jackie: It sounds like you've thought of everything.

Sherry: I've tried. When my parents died, it was a mess. They named me as executor because they knew I would follow their wishes exactly. But they didn't really finish things.

Jackie: What do you mean?

Sherry: They had an attorney make out their will, but they never signed it. They had a trust, but they never put the house in it.

Lydia: How do you put a house in a trust?

Sherry: You just take your trust to the courthouse or county administration building where you live, pay a fee, and change the name on the deed from yourself to your trust.

Lydia: That sounds easy enough.

Sherry: Easy if you do it, but more expensive and time consuming if you never get around to it.

Lydia: I assume everything will go to my kids, so I haven't put much thought into making it official.

Sherry: Then the state will decide for you.

Lydia: Oh no! I don't want that.

Sherry: Then you need to hop to it, young lady. I always say, "failing to plan is planning to fail."

Lydia realized she needed to meet with an attorney when she got home.

# Section 4

# Serving Others in Love

## *Reflection*

On the way home from the graduated care facility, Jackie stopped at the hardware store. As they moved along an end aisle, Bill walked out of the office and almost bumped into them.

Bill: Oh, excuse me. Hi Jackie, Lydia.

Lydia, *pleasantly surprised:* You remembered my name.

Bill: Yes, I wanted to invite you two ladies to a party at my house on Friday evening. Are you free?

Lydia shot Jackie a questioning look.

Jackie: What do you think, Lydia?

Lydia: Yes, we would love to.

Jackie blushed and Bill smiled broadly.

Bill: Good. You don't need to bring anything; just come around 5:30.

Jackie: Thank you, Bill.

Lydia: Bill, is this store one of your businesses?

Bill: No.

Larry, *from inside the office:* Well, it was. But he sold it to me a few years ago, and now we can't get rid of him.

They all laughed.

*From inside the office, sitting at her own desk, Larry's bookkeeper, Clara, looked over her glasses:* He's coaching Larry…he needs a *lot* of help!

They laughed again.

Larry, *walking out of the office:* Jackie, what can I help you with?

Jackie: I have a closet doorknob that used to open when I turned it either way. Now, it only opens when I turn it one way. Do you have any way to fix that?

Larry walked Jackie two aisles over while asking more questions.

Bill, *turning to Lydia:* How is Jackie really doing? She acts like everything is okay, but I'm concerned about her.

Lydia, *smiling into Bill's eyes:* She's lonely, Bill. Do you have any way to fix that?

## *Giving vs. Getting*

Jackie and Lydia were walking from the hardware store back down the street when out of the bakery stumbled Karla.

Karla, *immediately bursting into laughter:* Oh my, you caught me on my doughnut run. My one vice…well, one of my vices. *More laughter.*

Jackie: Karla, what do you have going on this afternoon? Do you want to come over to the house?

Karla: Oh Jackie, I'd love to, but I'm on the way to the hospital. Do you know Karen who comes to the soup kitchen?

Jackie: The one with the *really* long hair?

Karla: Yes, she is in the hospital and I'm going to spend some time with her.

Lydia: That's nice. Did she ask you to?

Karla: No, but can you imagine how it would feel to be in the hospital alone, with no one to come visit?

Lydia: That would be terrible.

Lydia realized she had never thought much about how other people felt. She had spent most of her life inside her own head. She had learned the skill of showing empathy which helped her in her sales work, but that had been mostly for show. Even though she might not admit it out loud, she didn't really care for other people very much. This trip opened her eyes to what that might look like, and she was getting excited about starting to care about, and for, other people. The questions now were who should she help, and how much time would she have?

Jackie, *continuing down the sidewalk:* That bakery smells so good.

Lydia: It's making me hungry.

Jackie: Are you up for pizza?

Lydia: I haven't gone out for pizza in…I don't know how long. Rick never wanted to spend the money. We would just find a frozen pizza on sale and heat it up at home.

Jackie: Well, this place is a classic.

They walked another block and turned to go inside. A bell rang as they opened the door.

James, the owner who had been mentored by Jackie's husband, Ron, saw Jackie, and came over to give her a big hug. She hugged him back.

James: Hello, Mrs. Powers. It's been a while since I've seen you.

Jackie: I know, James. This is my cousin, Lydia Barnes.

Lydia, *reaching out to shake his hand:* Hi James, nice to meet you.

James, *returning the handshake:* Nice to meet you, Mrs. Barnes. Table for two?

Jackie: Yes, please.

James took them over to a corner booth and seated them.

James: I believe this is your favorite.

Jackie: Yes, it is. Thank you.

James: Jenny will be right over to get your drinks and take your orders. It's on the house today.

Jackie: Oh no, James, you say that every time.

James: If it weren't for you and Ron, I wouldn't have this place. I'd probably be in jail somewhere. The least that I can do is cover your lunch.

Jackie: Thank you, James.

The bell over the door rang again as Bill walked in.

He noticed Jackie and Lydia in the corner and came over to say, "Hi."

Lydia: Hi Bill. Do you want to join us?

Bill, *looking at Jackie:* Are you sure? I don't want to intrude.

Jackie: You're welcome to join us, Bill.

Bill, *sliding into the booth next to Jackie and winking at Lydia:* Well, alright, then, if you insist, I will. Thank you.

Lydia: Bill, can I go back to your story? I'm curious as to why you sold so much of your real estate and so many of your businesses. Maybe I'm being too nosy?

Bill: No, that's a good question. There were several things that motivated me to sell off some assets. I had way more money than I needed, and I was getting greedy again.

Lydia: What do you mean again?

Bill: Remember when I said that when I was younger, I was wearing myself out to get more and more?

Lydia: Yes.

Bill: I kind of cooled off for a while after I met Janet. I started spending a lot of time with her when we were dating and slowed down my business pursuits.

Lydia: Okay.

Bill: But after we had been married a few years, and we started a family, I picked up where I left off and started getting aggressive again. I don't know if I was trying to impress her, or feeling responsible to provide for the family, or just being too greedy, or a combination of all those things.

Lydia: I see.

Bill: Anyway, she confronted me because she could see I was wearing myself out building more wealth and not spending much time with the family.

Jackie: Understandable.

Bill: Yes, but I didn't see it the same way as she did, so I ignored her cautions for a few years. I guess I didn't want to see it. I wanted to keep building my little empire.

Jackie: Oh, my.

Bill: But I started losing what little precious sleep I needed. I would wake up during the night making lists of things to do and worrying over things I couldn't control. And I was losing weight. That's when the light bulb went on. There was just too much on my plate. She was right.

Lydia: Heavy load.

Bill: Yep. So that's the first thing. The second thing is that I figured out how much our family actually needed to cover our expenses and still be able to give away half our income. We had more than what we needed for that.

Lydia: Nice problem to have.

Bill: I decided to start selling some stuff, but I didn't want to just get rid of it. I wanted to help some businesspeople the way Mrs. Porter helped me. So, I would keep my eyes open for a young person that was friendly and helpful. Then I would have a talk with them to see what their goals were. If they seemed to have some fire in their belly, and they were teachable, I would find a way to sell them some property, or one of my businesses, or both. This helped them get a financial head start, and it simplified my life eventually.

Lydia: Why not immediately?

Bill: Well, I would spend time with each person that was taking over a property or business—kind of showing them the ropes. This took more time than just running it myself, but over time, I also worked my way out of some jobs, so to speak.

Jackie: Is that what you're doing with Larry? At the hardware store?

Bill: Yep.

Lydia: That's really kind of you, Bill.

Bill: It's fun. I get to help some people and give some extra money away in the process.

Lydia: That's two reasons. Were there more?

Bill: Yes. My life is a lot simpler, and the phone is a lot quieter now. I used to be running strong all day long and have a few minutes to catch up with Janet before dropping dead asleep at night. I feel like I missed some of the years when our kids were growing up.

Jackie: There are probably a lot of people who run like that.

Bill: I did for a long time. But as I lightened my load, I started sleeping better. Janet and I started doing more things together and with the kids. It was a lot of fun. We got along well most of the time and I loved hanging out with them all. We were having a blast until…*Bill choked up, and tears started forming in his eyes.*

Jackie, *instinctively reaching out to hold his hand:* I'm sorry, Bill. It's hard, isn't it?

Then Jackie realized this could have been taken as more than a sympathetic gesture from a friend and started to pull back her hand, but Bill didn't let go.

Bill, *turning to look Jackie in the eyes:* Thank you.

Lydia, *sliding out of the booth:* Excuse me, I need to use the restroom.

# S.N.O.W.C.A.P

After a few minutes, Lydia returned from the restroom and Bill and Jackie were no longer holding hands, but they were talking freely.

Lydia, *at a natural break in the conversation:* Bill, why are you still working at all? You could be traveling and taking it easy, but you still seem very busy. Why not sell everything and just live off the money?

Bill: I move at a slower pace now, but I'm not sure I'll ever retire completely. It's too much fun to be productive and helpful. Now I work to build S.N.O.W.C.A.P.

Jackie: What's S.N.O.W.C.A.P.?

Bill: It's a small foundation Janet and I started.

Lydia: Is it for mountain exploration? Or environmental research?

Bill, *laughing gently:* No, that would be fun though. S.N.O.W.C.A.P. is an acronym. It stands for Sick, Naked (or poor), Orphans, Widows, Crippled, Aliens (refugees), and Prisoners. As you read through the Bible, these groups of people just keep showing up on God's heart. These are the people God wants us to care for--to help. He says that when we do things for these people it's like we are doing them for God, and I want to be rich toward God.

Lydia: What did you just say?

Bill: I want to be rich toward God.

Lydia: How does that work?

Bill: Jesus said that whatever we do for the S.N.O.W.C.A.P. people, or the vulnerable, it's like we are doing it for his brother or sister, and therefore, for him.

Lydia: I still don't get the connection.

Bill, *pausing:* Let's say I was driving along and saw some guy's car broken down beside the road. I pull over and give him a ride to his next stop and he thanks me. Then I forget all about it. But a week later, I receive a very nice thank you card in the mail with a big check inside. Come to find out, the father of the guy I helped is rich and famous. The card says how thankful this man is that I helped his son and I'm thinking, "Wow, am I glad I stopped to give that guy a ride!"

Lydia: You were lucky enough to stop and help the right person.

Bill: That's just it, when we help people in need, we are always lucky enough to help the right person. God is rich and famous, and he not only looks out for these people, but he rewards those who help them. By doing kind deeds, we become rich toward God. He says he'll repay us.

Lydia: Oh…I think I get it!

Bill: Most of us go through seasons of life when we need a helping hand. Our foundation works on creative ways to give people a hand up instead of a handout. I can't think of a more important work than this. We meet practical needs, and we become rich toward God in the process.

Lydia, *half joking:* Do you have any positions open at your foundation?

Bill: Actually, yes, we do. I have some great team members who help with accounting and investment management, but we need someone that can help raise funds…a salesperson, if you will.

Lydia, *as the pizza was arriving at their table:* Hmm. We should talk more about that sometime.

# *Hospitality*

Jackie and Lydia pulled up to Bill's house.

Lydia, *in surprise:* I thought he would have a bigger place.

Jackie: No, Bill's a pretty humble guy. He's not out to impress people.

Lydia: Rick and I were getting ready to buy a bigger house. I said it was so that we would have room for the kids to come home for the holidays.

Jackie: Yes?

Lydia: And that was *part* of it. But deep down, I wanted to keep up with some friends who live in a very posh neighborhood.

Jackie: Are you still planning to upgrade?

Lydia: No, it doesn't seem that important to me now.

Jackie: Hmm.

Lydia: Jackie, thank you for this week.

Jackie: It's been so good to have you here with me.

Lydia: Yes. I've really enjoyed getting to know you better as an adult. But I also mean the people you've introduced me to. It's been fascinating to meet so many people from so many backgrounds. It really helps put things in perspective. This was exactly what I needed. I still have some puzzles to solve, but I think I have a clearer idea of what this next year needs to look like for me.

Jackie: Aww…I'm so glad.

Lydia: Well, we should get inside. I think Bill is waiting for you.

Jackie: You mean *us*?

Lydia, *with a smirk:* No, I mean *you*!

## Recalibration

A couple of days later, as planned, Lydia departed for home. On the way, she pondered the conversations from her week at Jackie's place. She also replayed the weird experience from several weeks earlier. She concluded it was not only real, but unlike most dreams, it was meant to wake her up.

Though still terrified of dying, she thought some changes might help prepare her for the inevitable. She started mapping out what her life might look like with whatever time she had left.

She listed her house and sold it rather quickly, but instead of buying a larger one, she bought a smaller one closer to her children and closer to Jackie and Bill. The money left over from the house exchange she gave to her children. She enjoyed seeing them benefit from this gift while still alive.

Soon after that, she retired from her sales position and started volunteering part time to raise funds for Bill's foundation. The list of business associates she had accumulated provided a natural starting point, and Bill offered many additional contacts. She was able to raise several million dollars in donations for the foundation. It gave her deep satisfaction to be part of something bigger and more important than anything she had done before.

Between moving closer and working for the S.N.O.W.C.A.P. Foundation, she was able to travel regularly and see Jackie frequently, both of which brought her great joy.

A few months after returning home, following some routine blood work, she went to see her doctor for an annual exam. The doctor was more sober and less cheerful than normal, but before she said anything, Lydia knew.

Lydia: I have cancer, don't I?

Doctor: It looks that way. How did you know?

Lydia, *smiling slightly:* Well, I didn't have any symptoms, but let's just say I had a very clear sign.

Doctor, *concerned:* Lydia, this is a very aggressive form of cancer.

Lydia, *sobered suddenly:* Oh.

On her way home from the appointment, she recalled the night visit several months earlier. As frightened and panicked as she had been during the experience itself, with the warning being vague and surreal, now the warning was vivid and the experience itself seemed surreal and faded.

However, for the next few days she wrestled with deep depression. She didn't feel like getting out of bed, eating, or visiting anyone, so she didn't. She felt like she was in a deep, dark pit and wondered if this would be how she would spend her remaining days.

Suddenly, the ringing phone startled her. She wondered if she should answer it. She didn't want to talk to anyone, but she looked at the caller ID and saw that it was Jackson. She thought of how inspiring he had been to her.

Lydia, *picking up her phone:* Hello, Jackson?

Jackson: Hullo, Miss Lydia.

Lydia, *dully:* Jackson, it's good to hear from you.

Jackson, *obviously pleased:* Miss Lydia, it's so good to hear ya' boice.

Lydia, *blurting out coolly:* Jackson, I found out I have cancer. No one else knows. You are the first person I've told.

Jackson, *after a long pause:* Well, I'm mighty hono'd, Miss Lydia, dat ya' would tell me fust. How yo' holdin' up wit' de news?

Lydia, *flatly:* I've been depressed the last few days and I feel hopeless.

Jackson: I's sorry to hear dat, Miss Lydia. I truly am.

Lydia: I'm in a really dark place, Jackson.

Jackson: Oh my…I guess dat's why I's s'posed to call ya'. I read this verse and felt a hebby burden to call and share't wid ya'.

Lydia, *mildly reluctant and confused:* Share what?

Jackson: I been readin' in Mr. John's story 'bout Jesus. In chapta' 12, verse 46, he quotes Jesus, "I hab come inta de world as a light, so dat no one who believes in me should stay in da'kness."

I think the Laud want' me to call and share dis wid ya'.

Lydia: That's where I've been the last few days, in darkness.

No, Jackson, that's where I've been ever since my daddy lost his business. I decided God wasn't very good, and I've been drifting away from him ever since. It's been getting darker all the time. Now, it's like someone just blew out the last candle.

Jackson, *sniffling:* I's so sorry. Ya's hurtin' real bad. Can I's pray fo' ya', Miss Lydia.

Lydia: Please do.

Jackson, *through tears:* Laud, God Almighty. Ya' see Miss Lydia down in the pit o' darkness. How's she 'posed to' get out? Y's the God o' light. Can ya' shine some o' dat light on her right now? Show her de way out, please Laud. In the sweet name o' Jesus. 'men.

Lydia, *after a pause:* Jackson, I think I have an answer.

Jackson: Ya don't say?

Lydia: I've been alone, focusing on myself, and feeling sorry for myself.

Jackson: Jus' natur'l.

Lydia: Yes, but it hasn't been very helpful. As you were finishing up your prayer, an idea came to me.

Jackson: What's dat, Miss Lydia?

Lydia: I need to start looking for ways to help people!

Jackson: Now dat idea's packed full o' wisdom. Ya's helps od'r people and ya' can't he'p but feel better 'bout ya'self.

Lydia: Thank you for calling and listening, and for praying.

Jackson: Abs'lutely.

Oh, I hab an idea too, Miss Lydia.

Lydia: What is that?

Jackson: Ya' eve' make a tank ya' list?

Lydia: I'm not sure what that is.

Jackson: Ya' write down all de people and all de tings you be tankful fo'. Then ya' starts to writin' tank ya' notes and sendin' 'em out. Nex' ting ya' know, ya' hear back from a few dem people and ya' won't believe how good it make ya' feel. Ya' be singin' in no time.

Lydia, *brightening:* That's a great idea! Thank you, Jackson.

Jackson, *grinning and wiping his eyes with his shirtsleeve:* De pleasure's all mine, Miss Lydia. All mine. Thank ya', Laud.

O', Miss Lydia?

Lydia, *curiously:* Yes?

Jackson: One mo' ting.

Lydia: What is it?

Jackson: Ya' say you been driftin' away from the Laud fo' a long time. Ya' know de Laud, he be glad to' take ya' back right now.

Lydia: I've drifted a long way from the Lord. I was really angry when my dad lost his business. And I was *really* angry when my husband died. If I'm honest, I don't really like God very much.

Jackson: Dat's too bad, Miss Lydia, 'cause he lub ya' an awful lot.

Lydia, *with swelling sobs:* Jackson, I feel like he's talking through you. I know what you're saying is true, but I've run away and tried to carry my life by myself. It's a heavy load, Jackson. It feels so heavy right now, I'm not so sure he would take me back.

Jackson: Jesus, he say, "Come to me, all yo' who weary an' burdened, an' I will gib yo' rest…Fo' my yoke's easy an' my burden's light."

He's sayin' dat to ya', Miss Lydia. Ya' ready to hand it over to him?

Lydia, *still sobbing:* Yes, part of me wants to, and part of me doesn't know if I can trust him.

Jackson: You want to tell him that right now?

Lydia: Right now?

Jackson: Yes'm.

Lydia: God…I've been so mad at you…You took my daddy's business away…and my husband away. I didn't think I could ever trust you because I thought you were mean and angry.

*Pause.*

Jackson, *reassuringly:* Git' all out, Miss Lydia. He knows ana'way.

Lydia, *through tears:* I didn't think I could trust you until I met Jackson. Lord, he's like you, isn't he? You have been watching me and wanting me to come back to you all this time.

*More sobbing.* I'm sorry I didn't believe you were good. I'm sorry I've run away and tried to control my own life. I need you. I need to trust you. You *are* good. You *do* care. Will you forgive me and take me back?

Jackson, *involuntarily:* O' course, Miss Lydia, he'll take ya' back. He jus' been waitin' on de front po'ch fo' ya' to come home.

Lydia, *after blowing her nose:* Heavenly Father, I want to come home. I want to follow you with whatever time you give me. Amen.

Jackson, *wiping his eyes again:* Dat's de way, Miss Lydia.

Lydia: Jackson!

Jackson: Yes'm?

Lydia: I feel happy and free, like the sun just came out from the clouds.

Jackson: Jus' like he say.

Lydia: I don't know how I could ever repay you.

Jackson: Ya' don't owe me nuttin', Miss Lydia. Ya' my friend. De Laud say, "Call ya' friend, Miss Lydia," an' I say, "Yes, Laud." It's dat plain and simple. Nows I know why.

Lydia: Thank you, friend.

Jackson, *grinning through tears:* Ya' mighty welcome, Miss Lydia. Mighty welcome.

## A New Focus

As soon as she hung up, Lydia started her thank you list, beginning with Jackson, then Jackie, then God. She filled two pages of names and opportunities in her life. Then she went to the store and bought some thank you cards. The first three notes were in the mailbox before she went to bed that night, and she couldn't wait to send more. She wrote to her schoolteachers, family members, and former co-workers. Her enthusiasm grew as she thought of more people that had made a difference in her life. Her joy grew immensely as she heard back from several of these people.

She found her childhood Bible and started reading it every morning. This time of reading, and the prayers that naturally welled up in response, became very precious to her.

Over the next few months, Lydia found herself giving more and more money away to individuals and organizations in need. It had always brought a little satisfaction to save money and see her savings grow. It never occurred to her that giving money away and seeing her accounts shrink could give her much deeper satisfaction. She was not just spending her money; she felt for the first time that she was investing her money and her life in ways that really mattered.

She spent time visiting her kids in their homes. She especially enjoyed a week of cleaning, cooking, shopping, and organizing as her daughter-in-law, Cherise, delivered a new baby girl into their family. This brought such deep joy to Lydia, but it was mixed with sadness that she would not likely see this girl grow up and start her own family. But she treasured her family and her minutes with them like never before.

In her new house, she had a basement apartment for her kids to stay when they came to visit her. In between these visits, she rented this space to temporary guests. Over the months, she met some fascinating people. Ironically, Lydia's fear of being robbed faded as she had more people coming and going from her house.

Lydia started volunteering in her spare hours. She would often collapse into bed at night exhausted. But she felt it was a good tired as it helped her sleep more deeply and restfully than she had since childhood.

This tiredness, however, did not keep her from calling Jackson every Sunday night. They would talk about what they were learning and doing. It was the highlight of her week.

And she followed Janice's advice to get involved in a church nearby. She met several new friends there, including a couple that became very close very quickly. And during the worship services, for the first time in her life, she felt like she was in God's presence. It was changing her heart and her perspective on everything.

One especially meaningful time was when a single mom, Laura, came to stay with Lydia. Lydia let her and her two young boys stay with her for almost a month while Laura was in a housing and job transition.

While Laura's family was there, Lydia would often fix supper for them, and she would help Laura with laundry and getting the boys ready for bed. After the boys were down, Lydia would pour a cup of hot chocolate for Laura, and the two women would talk.

Laura's mother had never taken the time to teach Laura the life lessons Lydia was sharing with her. These lessons had a very deep and positive impact on Laura. She was so grateful for the place to stay, but even more grateful for how Lydia had poured into her life in practical and personal ways.

# Epilogue

Jackie and Bill started seeing each other more often. He would take her out on dates, or they would get together with friends to play games or watch a movie. They continued volunteering at the mission and Bill also joined her on the weekly visits with friends at the graduated care facility. They walked and talked. They read books together. She felt her guard dropping as her attraction, affection, and trust grew toward Bill. With eagerness, she began anticipating the next time she would see Bill. She wanted to be with him more and more. Without realizing it, she had given her heart to him.

One evening, about four months later, Bill took Jackie to her favorite Mexican restaurant. They had a good time talking about a variety of topics, but Bill seemed a little more nervous than usual. After the main course, the server brought out dessert. Jackie was puzzled since they had not ordered dessert, until she noticed a ring sparkling at her from the top of the deep-fried ice cream. The server left promptly, but when the staff saw her nodding her head and hugging Bill, the Mariachi band came alongside their table and sang a traditional love song. She was crying with joy.

A couple of months later, Lydia was standing beside Jackie as her matron of honor. The family retold happy and humorous stories throughout the day, along with hugs and laughter. Lydia marveled at how comfortable Jackie and Bill seemed together. She, of course, gave herself partial credit for her gentle nudges that helped make it happen. Lydia was pleasantly surprised to reconnect with Karla and Janice as they talked and laughed together during the wedding reception. She also met Roger, Karla's boyfriend, and Jerry, Janice's husband.

Lydia was overflowing with joy for her cousin, Jackie, for several weeks. But then she heard the news about Jackson. He was gone. How could this be possible? He was so full of life. She had just talked to him the week before. The sharp pain of grief crushed her glittery bubble of joy, turning it into heavy imploding gloom.

A few days later, she and Jackie cried all the way through his funeral. Afterwards, Jackson's youngest daughter came up to Jackie and Lydia.

Felicia, *through tears:* Are you Miss Jackie and Miss Lydia?

Together, *nodding:* Yes, we are.

Felicia: My daddy told me you were two of the best friends he ever had.

This is Daddy's Bible. Look here in John 12. Here's Lydia's name next to verse 46. And here are some of the many tear stains in his Bible.

They had just regained their composure before her comment started a new fountain of tears. They held Felicia and sobbed together. After a couple minutes, they let go, and stared at each other in wonder.

Lydia: He changed my life. You are a blessed girl to have a daddy like that.

Felicia: Yes, ma'am, I am.

Jackie: He was a wonderful man. I will never forget him.

They expressed their condolences to each other as well as how grateful they were to meet one another.

☙ ❧

Over the next few months, Lydia kept visiting her kids, volunteering, and giving money away, but she felt more tired all the time, and started to feel pain in different parts of her body. She had kept in touch with her doctor, and they both knew what was coming. But her fear of death was gradually being replaced with nervousness, then with a growing sense of peace, and finally, with anticipation.

Her last few weeks she had a parade of visitors whose lives she had impacted, including her son, neighbors, former co-workers, and many new friends. Her daughter and her cousin, Jackie, came to stay with her for the final week. They fed her and cared for her as her strength diminished.

She slept more frequently. In between, Lydia told Jackie how much the visit had meant to her a year earlier, and how much it had changed her life. They shared stories from childhood and talked about the afterlife. They also sang, prayed, and cried together. It was another highlight of the year for Lydia to have her daughter and her cousin with her during this time.

She also received a surprise visit from Laura, who had stayed with her for a month. Laura knew Lydia's time was short and she wanted to thank Lydia for how much she had given her and the boys. She wasn't sure how to express her gratitude, but as she stumbled along, Laura made a comment that filled Lydia with astonishment.

Laura: Lydia, you're so rich in a God sort of way.

Nothing she could have said would have hit Lydia any harder. Lydia didn't have the strength to laugh, but she closed her eyes and fell asleep with a smile on her face.

Three days later was the anniversary of her visitor. Lydia slept most of the day. But she woke for a few minutes in the evening, while Jackie and Lydia's daughter were chatting quietly. Lydia reached out her chilly hand and they both moved closer to her bed and held it. She mustered up the energy to speak, but they had to lean in close to hear her whisper, "I love you both." She paused, then said, "I am so rich."

She closed her eyes, and a few moments later, she was gone. She left some money to her kids and charities, but she left a legacy of even greater impact because the last year of her life she lived like never before.

At her funeral, her pastor explained that her last year she was rich toward God because she practiced Legacy Living.

# Section 5

# Applications to Life

# Or Was It a Dream?

**Wisdom from the Word**

Luke 12:15-21: 15 Then he [Jesus] said to them, "Watch out! Be on your
guard against all kinds of greed; life does not consist in an abundance
of possessions."

16 And he told them this parable: "The ground of a certain rich man
yielded an abundant harvest. 17 He thought to himself, 'What shall I do?
I have no place to store my crops.'

18 "Then he said, 'This is what I'll do. I will tear down my barns and
build bigger ones, and there I will store my surplus grain. 19 And I'll say
to myself, "You have plenty of grain laid up for many years. Take life
easy; eat, drink and be merry."'

20 "But God said to him, 'You fool! This very night your life will be
demanded from you. Then who will get what you have prepared for
yourself?'

21 "This is how it will be with whoever stores up things for themselves
but is not rich toward God."

Luke 12:35-40: 35 "Be dressed ready for service and keep your lamps
burning, 36 like servants waiting for their master to return from a
wedding banquet, so that when he comes and knocks they can
immediately open the door for him. 37 It will be good for those servants
whose master finds them watching when he comes. Truly I tell you, he
will dress himself to serve, will have them recline at the table and will
come and wait on them. 38 It will be good for those servants whose
master finds them ready, even if he comes in the middle of the night or
toward daybreak. 39 But understand this: If the owner of the house had
known at what hour the thief was coming, he would not have let his
house be broken into. 40 You also must be ready, because the Son of
Man will come at an hour when you do not expect him."

ꟹ ꟹ

James 4:13-15: [13] Now listen, you who say, "Today or tomorrow we will go to this or that city, spend a year there, carry on business and make money." [14] Why, you do not even know what will happen tomorrow. What is your life? You are a mist that appears for a little while and then vanishes. [15] Instead, you ought to say, "If it is the Lord's will, we will live and do this or that."

## Questions for Reflection

How long will you live?

What are some benefits of remembering this?

How do you, or could you, remind yourself that life is uncertain?

What do you do, or could you start doing, to celebrate each day?

# *Hilarious Giving*

**Wisdom from the Word**

Acts 20:34-35: [34] "You yourselves know that these hands of mine have supplied my own needs and the needs of my companions. [35] In everything I did, I showed you that by this kind of hard work we must help the weak, remembering the words the Lord Jesus himself said: 'It is more blessed to give than to receive.'"

ଓ ଓ

2 Corinthians 9:6-8: [6] Remember this: Whoever sows sparingly will also reap sparingly, and whoever sows generously will also reap generously. [7] Each of you should give what you have decided in your heart to give, not reluctantly or under compulsion, for God loves a cheerful *[hilarious]* giver. [8] And God is able to bless you abundantly, so that in all things at all times, having all that you need, you will abound in every good work.

ଓ ଓ

2 Corinthians 9:11-12: [11] You will be enriched in every way so that you can be generous on every occasion, and through us your generosity will result in thanksgiving to God.

[12] This service that you perform is not only supplying the needs of the Lord's people but is also overflowing in many expressions of thanks to God.

ଓ ଓ

**Quotes from the Author**

How much we accumulate does not measure how rich we are. It only measures our ability to accumulate, or maybe, to hoard.

Having wealth is one thing. Having an abundant life is something else.

Being rich doesn't necessarily mean your bank account is full. It means your life is overflowing.

A rich person gives no matter how much he or she has.

Giving makes us richer than getting. This isn't a math principle; it's a spiritual principle and a psychological phenomenon. It isn't expected, but it works.

The opposite of a rich person is not a poor person; it's a greedy person.

The longer we hold onto money, the stickier it gets.

It's good to accumulate, but what is the *so-that…?*

God did not design resources to be hoarded, but to be enjoyed and shared.

**Questions for Reflection**

Is giving more of a duty or a delight for you personally?

Do you know why?

What are some of the benefits of giving?

What else could you give away?

What could you change to be able to give more away?

What charities are you the most passionate about because of personal experience or belief?

What charities do you believe are doing the most good for people?

What charities do you believe are the most strategic for building God's kingdom?

# *Richly Loved*

**Wisdom from the Word**

Psalm 139

1 You have searched me, LORD,
and you know me.
2 You know when I sit and when I rise;
you perceive my thoughts from afar.
3 You discern my going out and my lying down;
you are familiar with all my ways.
4 Before a word is on my tongue
you, LORD, know it completely.
5 You hem me in behind and before,
and you lay your hand upon me.
6 Such knowledge is too wonderful for me,
too lofty for me to attain.
7 Where can I go from your Spirit?
Where can I flee from your presence?
8 If I go up to the heavens, you are there;
if I make my bed in the depths, you are there.
9 If I rise on the wings of the dawn,
if I settle on the far side of the sea,
10 even there your hand will guide me,
your right hand will hold me fast.
11 If I say, "Surely the darkness will hide me
and the light become night around me,"
12 even the darkness will not be dark to you;
the night will shine like the day,
for darkness is as light to you. 13 For you created my inmost being;
you knit me together in my mother's womb.
14 I praise you because I am fearfully and wonderfully made;
your works are wonderful,
I know that full well.
15 My frame was not hidden from you
when I was made in the secret place,
when I was woven together in the depths of the earth.

16 Your eyes saw my unformed body;
all the days ordained for me were written in your book
before one of them came to be.
17 How precious to me are your thoughts, God!
How vast is the sum of them!
18 Were I to count them,
they would outnumber the grains of sand—
when I awake, I am still with you.
19 If only you, God, would slay the wicked!
Away from me, you who are bloodthirsty!
20 They speak of you with evil intent;
your adversaries misuse your name.
21 Do I not hate those who hate you, LORD,
and abhor those who are in rebellion against you?
22 I have nothing but hatred for them;
I count them my enemies.
23 Search me, God, and know my heart;
test me and know my anxious thoughts.
24 See if there is any offensive way in me,
and lead me in the way everlasting.

Jeremiah 31:3: [3] The LORD appeared to us in the past, saying: "I have loved you with an everlasting love; I have drawn you with unfailing kindness."

John 14:23: [23] Jesus replied, "Anyone who loves me will obey my teaching. My Father will love them, and we will come to them and make our home with them."

John 3:16: [16] "For God so loved the world that he gave his one and only Son, that whoever believes in him shall not perish but have eternal life."

1 John 3:1: [1] See what great love the Father has lavished on us, that we should be called children of God!

ᴓ ᴓ

1 John 3:16: [16] This is how we know what love is: Jesus Christ laid down his life for us. And we ought to lay down our lives for our brothers and sisters.

ᴓ ᴓ

**Questions for Reflection**

Out of all the billions of people alive today, do you believe God knows you personally?

Why or why not?

Do you believe he loves you deeply?

What, if anything, would be different if you sincerely believed this?

How would this change your relationship with him?

How might this change your relationships with other people?

## *Richly Provided*

**Wisdom from the Word**

Matthew 6:11: [11] "Give us today our daily bread."

ঔ ৩

Matthew 14:17-21: [17] "We have here only five loaves of bread and two fish," they answered.

[18] "Bring them here to me," he said. [19] And he directed the people to sit down on the grass. Taking the five loaves and the two fish and looking up to heaven, he gave thanks and broke the loaves. Then he gave them to the disciples, and the disciples gave them to the people. [20] They all ate and were satisfied, and the disciples picked up twelve basketfuls of broken pieces that were left over. [21] The number of those who ate was about five thousand men, besides women and children.

ঔ ৩

Luke 12:22-31: [22] Then Jesus said to his disciples: "Therefore I tell you, do not worry about your life, what you will eat; or about your body, what you will wear. [23] For life is more than food, and the body more than clothes.

[24] "Consider the ravens: They do not sow or reap, they have no storeroom or barn; yet God feeds them. And how much more valuable you are than birds! [25] Who of you by worrying can add a single hour to your life? [26] Since you cannot do this very little thing, why do you worry about the rest?

27 “Consider how the wildflowers grow. They do not labor or spin. Yet
I tell you, not even Solomon in all his splendor was dressed like one of
these. 28 If that is how God clothes the grass of the field, which is here
today, and tomorrow is thrown into the fire, how much more will he
clothe you—you of little faith! 29 And do not set your heart on what
you will eat or drink; do not worry about it. 30 For the pagan world runs
after all such things, and your Father knows that you need them. 31 But
seek his kingdom, and these things will be given to you as well.”

John 10:10: 10 “The thief [Satan] comes only to steal and kill and destroy; I [Jesus] have come that they may have life and have it to the full [abundant, overflowing life].”

1 Timothy 6:17: 17 Command those who are rich in this present world not to be arrogant nor to put their hope in wealth, which is so uncertain, but to put their hope in God, who richly provides us with everything for our enjoyment.

### Questions for Reflection

How rich would you say you are compared to ten years ago?

How rich would you say you are by American standards?

How rich would you say you are by worldwide standards?

How rich would you say you are by historical standards?

Is there anything you lack that really matters?

What makes you the richest?

## *A.S.K. Principle*

**Wisdom from the Word**

Matthew 6:8: [8] "…for your Father knows what you need before you ask him."

ᘛ ᘚ

Matthew 7:7-8: [7] "Ask, and it will be given to you; seek, and you will find; knock, and it will be opened to you. [8] For everyone who asks receives, and he who seeks finds, and to him who knocks it will be opened."

ᘛ ᘚ

Luke 11:11-13: [11] "Which of you fathers, if your son asks for a fish, will give him a snake instead? [12] Or if he asks for an egg, will give him a scorpion? [13] If you then, though you are evil, know how to give good gifts to your children, how much more will your Father in heaven give the Holy Spirit to those who ask him!"

ᘛ ᘚ

John 14:13-14: [13] "And I will do whatever you ask in my name, so that the Father may be glorified in the Son. [14] You may ask me for anything in my name, and I will do it."

ᘛ ᘚ

1 John 5:14: [14] This is the confidence we have in approaching God: that if we ask anything according to his will, he hears us.

ᘛ ᘚ

**Questions for Reflection**

Do you believe God is aware of your needs?

Do you believe he hears you when you pray?

Do you believe God answers prayer?

Do you believe God answer your prayers?

Are there things you need that you have not asked God for yet?

Why not?

Would you like to ask him now?

# *Richly Protected*

**Wisdom from the Word**

Psalm 18:3-19: 3 I called to the LORD, who is worthy of praise,
and I have been saved from my enemies.
4 The cords of death entangled me;
the torrents of destruction overwhelmed me.
5 The cords of the grave coiled around me;
the snares of death confronted me.
6 In my distress I called to the LORD;
I cried to my God for help.
From his temple he heard my voice;
my cry came before him, into his ears.
7 The earth trembled and quaked,
and the foundations of the mountains shook;
they trembled because he was angry.
8 Smoke rose from his nostrils;
consuming fire came from his mouth,
burning coals blazed out of it.
9 He parted the heavens and came down;
dark clouds were under his feet.
10 He mounted the cherubim and flew;
he soared on the wings of the wind.
11 He made darkness his covering, his canopy around him—
the dark rain clouds of the sky.
12 Out of the brightness of his presence clouds advanced,
with hailstones and bolts of lightning.
13 The LORD thundered from heaven;
the voice of the Most High resounded.
14 He shot his arrows and scattered the enemy,
with great bolts of lightning he routed them.
15 The valleys of the sea were exposed
and the foundations of the earth laid bare
at your rebuke, LORD,
at the blast of breath from your nostrils.
16 He reached down from on high and took hold of me;
he drew me out of deep waters.

17 He rescued me from my powerful enemy,
from my foes, who were too strong for me.
18 They confronted me in the day of my disaster,
but the LORD was my support.
19 He brought me out into a spacious place;
he rescued me because he delighted in me.

Psalm 91:1-16: 1 Whoever dwells in the shelter of the Most High
will rest in the shadow of the Almighty.
2 I will say of the LORD, "He is my refuge and my fortress,
my God, in whom I trust."

3 Surely he will save you
from the fowler's snare
and from the deadly pestilence.
4 He will cover you with his feathers,
and under his wings you will find refuge;
his faithfulness will be your shield and rampart.
5 You will not fear the terror of night,
nor the arrow that flies by day,
6 nor the pestilence that stalks in the darkness,
nor the plague that destroys at midday.
7 A thousand may fall at your side,
ten thousand at your right hand,
but it will not come near you.
8 You will only observe with your eyes
and see the punishment of the wicked.

9 If you say, "The LORD is my refuge,"
and you make the Most High your dwelling,
10 no harm will overtake you,
no disaster will come near your tent.
11 For he will command his angels concerning you
to guard you in all your ways;
12 they will lift you up in their hands,
so that you will not strike your foot against a stone.
13 You will tread on the lion and the cobra;
you will trample the great lion and the serpent.

14 "Because he loves me," says the LORD, "I will rescue him;
I will protect him, for he acknowledges my name.
15 He will call on me, and I will answer him;
I will be with him in trouble,
I will deliver him and honor him.
16 With long life I will satisfy him
and show him my salvation."

**Questions for Reflection**

Are you naturally fearful or confident most of the time?

Why?

How often would you say you feel fearful?

What triggers fear in you?

When, if ever, do you feel safe and secure?

Do you think God, or some of his angels, are looking out for you?

Why or why not?

If he allows you to go through something difficult, is it because he doesn't notice, or care?

How has he used difficult experiences in your life for good?

If hard times (like disappointment, sickness, pain, loss, frustration, rejection, etc.) bring me closer to God, then aren't these things my friends?

# Contentment

## Wisdom from the Word

Job 1:21: [21] … and [Job] said: "Naked I came from my mother's womb, and naked I will depart. The LORD gave and the LORD has taken away; may the name of the LORD be praised."

Philippians 4:11-12: [11] I [Paul] am not saying this because I am in need, for I have learned to be content whatever the circumstances. I know what it is to be in need, and I know what it is to have plenty. [12] I have learned the secret of being content in any and every situation, whether well fed or hungry, whether living in plenty or in want.

1 Timothy 6:7-11: [7] For we brought nothing into the world, and we can take nothing out of it. [8] But if we have food and clothing, we will be content with that. [9] People who want to get rich fall into temptation and a trap and into many foolish and harmful desires that plunge men into ruin and destruction. [10] For the love of money is a root of all kinds of evil. Some people, eager for money, have wandered from the faith and pierced themselves with many griefs. [11] But you, man of God, flee from all this, and pursue righteousness, godliness, faith, love, endurance and gentleness.

Hebrews 13:5: [5] Keep your lives free from the love of money and be content with what you have, because God has said, "Never will I leave you; never will I forsake you."

2 Peter 1:3: [3] His divine power has given us everything we need for life and godliness through our knowledge of him who called us by his own glory and goodness.

☙ ❧

**Questions for Reflection**

Does the word, "contented" describe you well?

How often are you content?

If you are not now, what would it take to make you content?

Is that the real answer…would it really work?

Do you like it when people thank you?

Do you consistently notice and thank others who do things for you?

How grateful would God say you are toward him?

How grateful would other people say you are toward them?

# *Dying is the Best Place to Start*

**Wisdom from the Word**

Psalm 23:4: [4] Even though I walk through the valley of the shadow of death, I will fear no evil, for you are with me; your rod and your staff, they comfort me.

☙ ❧

Matthew 10:28: [28] "Do not be afraid of those who kill the body but cannot kill the soul. Rather, be afraid of the One who can destroy both soul and body in hell."

☙ ❧

Luke 9:23: [23] Then he said to them all: "Whoever wants to be my disciple must deny themselves and take up their cross daily and follow me."

☙ ❧

2 Corinthians 5:15: [15] And he died for all, that those who live should no longer live for themselves but for him who died for them and was raised again.

☙ ❧

Galatians 2:20: [20] "I have been crucified with Christ. It is no longer I who live, but Christ who lives in me. And the life I now live in the flesh I live by faith in the Son of God, who loved me and gave himself for me."

☙ ❧

**Questions for Reflection**

What do you want people to say at your funeral?

Is this likely to happen based on your life so far?

Why or why not?

What would you need to change to make people sincerely say the things you want to be true of your life?

For example, if you would start__________________________

What do you want God to say when you stand before him?

Is this likely?

What do you think it means to live for God?

For that to be true of you, what needs to change in your life?

What do you think God is waiting for from you?

What are you waiting for to change?

# *Where is Your Treasure?*

**Wisdom from the Word**

Matthew 6:19: [19] "Do not lay up for yourselves treasures on earth, where moth and rust destroy and where thieves break in and steal."

☙ ❧

Matthew 6:21: [21] "For where your treasure is, there your heart will be also."

☙ ❧

Matthew 19:21: [21] Jesus said to him, "If you would be perfect, go, sell what you possess and give to the poor, and you will have treasure in heaven; and come, follow me."

☙ ❧

Luke 12:32-34: [32] "Do not be afraid, little flock, for your Father has been pleased to give you the kingdom. [33] Sell your possessions and give to the poor. Provide purses for yourselves that will not wear out, a treasure in heaven that will never fail, where no thief comes near and no moth destroys. [34] For where your treasure is, there your heart will be also."

☙ ❧

1 Timothy 6:17-19: [17] Command those who are rich in this present world not to be arrogant nor to put their hope in wealth, which is so uncertain, but to put their hope in God, who richly provides us with everything for our enjoyment. [18] Command them to do good, to be rich in good deeds, and to be generous and willing to share. [19] In this way they will lay up treasure for themselves as a firm foundation for the coming age, so that they may take hold of the life that is truly life.

☙ ❧

**Questions for Reflection**

How many different forms of treasures do you have?

In what form is most of your treasure?

Do you spend more time thinking about treasure in heaven or on earth?

Do you spend more time building treasure in heaven or on earth?

What do you think it means that we will inherit the kingdom?

What kind of treasure do you speculate we will receive from God?

# Rich Toward God

**Wisdom from the Word**

Proverbs 19:17: [17] Whoever is kind to the poor lends to the LORD, and he will reward them for what they have done.

ଓ ଃ

Matthew 6:24: [24] "No one can serve two masters. Either you will hate the one and love the other, or you will be devoted to the one and despise the other. You cannot serve both God and money."

ଓ ଃ

Mark 9:41: [41] "Truly I [Jesus] tell you, anyone who gives you a cup of water in my name because you belong to the Messiah will certainly not lose their reward."

ଓ ଃ

Luke 6:38: [38] "Give, and it will be given to you. A good measure, pressed down, shaken together and running over, will be poured into your lap. For with the measure you use, it will be measured to you."

ଓ ଃ

Luke 12:20-21: [20] "But God said to him, 'You fool! This very night your life will be demanded from you. Then who will get what you have prepared for yourself?'

[21] "This is how it will be with whoever stores up things for themselves but is not rich toward God."

ଓ ଃ

(Parable of the Talents) Matthew 25:19-21: [19] "After a long time the master of those servants returned and settled accounts with them. [20] The man who had received five bags of gold brought the other five. 'Master,' he said, 'you entrusted me with five bags of gold. See, I have gained five more.'

[21] "His master replied, 'Well done, good and faithful servant! You have been faithful with a few things; I will put you in charge of many things. Come and share your master's happiness!'"

## Questions for Reflection

What makes a person rich?

What makes a person "rich toward God?"

What makes a person poor toward God?

How "rich toward God" would you say you are right now?

What would make you richer than you are now?

What changes can you make in your life to move in this direction?

# Assigning Where Things Go

**Wisdom from the Word**

Proverbs 13:22: [22] A good person leaves an inheritance for their children's children, but a sinner's wealth is stored up for the righteous.

ଓ ଓ

Proverbs 15:22: [22] Plans fail for lack of counsel, but with many advisers they succeed.

ଓ ଓ

Proverbs16:1,3,9: [1] To humans belong the plans of the heart, but from the LORD comes the proper answer of the tongue.

[3] Commit to the LORD whatever you do, and he will establish your plans.

[9] In their hearts humans plan their course, but the LORD establishes their steps.

ଓ ଓ

Ecclesiastes 7:11: [11] Wisdom, like an inheritance, is a good thing and benefits those who see the sun.

ଓ ଓ

John 19:26-27: [26] When Jesus saw his mother there, and the disciple whom he loved standing nearby, he said to her, "Woman, here is your son," [27] and to the disciple, "Here is your mother." From that time on, this disciple took her into his home.

ଓ ଓ

**Questions for Reflection**

Who will get your stuff?

Have you spelled this out in writing?

Either **state** this in a **will** or **trust**,<br>or else **trust** that the **state will**.

What kinds of end-of-life medical treatment do you want or not want?

Have you put this in writing and communicated it to your loved ones?

This is usually in the form of a **living will**,<br>which is not the same document as the will used to distribute assets.

It is also accompanied by two **power of attorney** documents,<br>one for business matters and one for health care matters.

These documents authorize named individuals to represent you<br>and carry out your wishes in case of disability.

Legacy Living includes preparing not only for your best future, but also that of others, such as your heirs.

Have you written any kind of message outlining your feelings and hopes toward your heirs, your values, your parting message?

How much would it have meant to you to receive something like this?

How long would it take to do this?

How much would this mean to them?

# *Giving vs. Getting*

**Wisdom from the Word**

Exodus 20:15: [15] "You shall not steal."

Matthew 19:21: [21] Jesus answered, "If you want to be perfect, go, sell your possessions and give to the poor, and you will have treasure in heaven. Then come, follow me."

Luke 16:9-11: [9] "I tell you, use worldly wealth to gain friends for yourselves, so that when it is gone, you will be welcomed into eternal dwellings.

[10] "Whoever can be trusted with very little can also be trusted with much, and whoever is dishonest with very little will also be dishonest with much. [11] So if you have not been trustworthy in handling worldly wealth, who will trust you with true riches?"

Galatians 6:10: [10] Therefore, as we have opportunity, let us do good to all people, especially to those who belong to the family of believers.

Ephesians 4:28: [28] Anyone who has been stealing must steal no longer, but must work, doing something useful with their own hands, that they may have something to share with those in need.

1 Timothy 6:9-10: [9] Those who want to get rich fall into temptation and a trap and into many foolish and harmful desires that plunge people into ruin and destruction. [10] For the love of money is a root of all kinds of evil. Some people, eager for money, have wandered from the faith and pierced themselves with many griefs.

☙ ❧

**Questions for Reflection**

Do you feel good when you help others or give them gifts?

Why do you suppose that is the case?

How many reasons can you come up with to validate the quote, "It is more blessed to give than receive"?

Has it ever made your day to make someone else's day?

What are some ways to do this?

Why not do this every day?

If you did, how much richer do you think your life would be?

# Multiplying vs. Consuming

**Wisdom from the Word**

Genesis 1:28a KJV: 28 And God blessed them, and God said unto them,
“Be fruitful, and multiply, and replenish the earth, and subdue it.”

Matthew 25:14-30: 14 “Again, it will be like a man going on a journey,
who called his servants and entrusted his wealth to them. 15 To one he
gave five bags of gold, to another two bags, and to another one bag,
each according to his ability. Then he went on his journey. 16 The man
who had received five bags of gold went at once and put his money to
work and gained five bags more. 17 So also, the one with two bags of
gold gained two more. 18 But the man who had received one bag went
off, dug a hole in the ground and hid his master’s money.

19 “After a long time the master of those servants returned and settled
accounts with them. 20 The man who had received five bags of gold
brought the other five. ‘Master,’ he said, ‘you entrusted me with five
bags of gold. See, I have gained five more.’

21 “His master replied, ‘Well done, good and faithful servant! You have
been faithful with a few things; I will put you in charge of many things.
Come and share your master’s happiness!’

22 “The man with two bags of gold also came. ‘Master,’ he said, ‘you
entrusted me with two bags of gold; see, I have gained two more.’

23 “His master replied, ‘Well done, good and faithful servant! You have
been faithful with a few things; I will put you in charge of many things.
Come and share your master’s happiness!’

[24] "Then the man who had received one bag of gold came. 'Master,' he said, 'I knew that you are a hard man, harvesting where you have not sown and gathering where you have not scattered seed. [25] So I was afraid and went out and hid your gold in the ground. See, here is what belongs to you.'

[26] "His master replied, 'You wicked, lazy servant! So you knew that I harvest where I have not sown and gather where I have not scattered seed? [27] Well then, you should have put my money on deposit with the bankers, so that when I returned I would have received it back with interest.

[28] "'So take the bag of gold from him and give it to the one who has ten bags. [29] For whoever has will be given more, and they will have an abundance. Whoever does not have, even what they have will be taken from them. [30] And throw that worthless servant outside, into the darkness, where there will be weeping and gnashing of teeth.'"

Mark 10:28-30: [28] Then Peter spoke up, "We have left everything to follow you!"

[29] "Truly I tell you," Jesus replied, "no one who has left home or brothers or sisters or mother or father or children or fields for me and the gospel [30] will fail to receive a hundred times as much in this present age: homes, brothers, sisters, mothers, children and fields—along with persecutions—and in the age to come eternal life.

**Questions for Reflection**

We are told to, "Be fruitful and multiply" by God. At what age do you think he wants us to stop doing this?

Where does the idea of retirement come from?

Why do we think it is a good idea to work for 30 or 40 years, then stop?

Why do we think it is a good idea to accumulate savings for 30 to 40 years, then deplete savings for 30 to 40 years?

How does this help us to be good stewards?

Have you ever thought about finding work you would love to keep doing, even part-time, for as long as possible?

Have you ever had someone calculate the financial impact it could have on your family and on the kingdom if you kept accumulating and giving as long as possible?

## Wisdom from the Word

### Sick

Ezekiel 34:4: [4] "You have not strengthened the weak or healed the sick or bound up the injured. You have not brought back the strays or searched for the lost…."

ꕥ ꕥ

Matthew 4:23: [23] Jesus went throughout Galilee, teaching in their synagogues, preaching the good news of the kingdom, and healing every disease and sickness among the people.

ꕥ ꕥ

James 5:14-15: [14] Is any one of you sick? He should call the elders of the church to pray over him and anoint him with oil in the name of the Lord. [15] And the prayer offered in faith will make the sick person well; the Lord will raise him up. If he has sinned, he will be forgiven.

### Naked

Isaiah 58:7: [7] "Is it not to share your food with the hungry and to provide the poor wanderer with shelter—when you see the naked, to clothe him, and not to turn away from your own flesh and blood?"

ꕥ ꕥ

Ezekiel 18:16: [16] "He does not oppress anyone or require a pledge for a loan. He does not commit robbery but gives his food to the hungry and provides clothing for the naked."

## Orphans

Psalm 82:3: [3] Defend the cause of the weak and fatherless; maintain the rights of the poor and oppressed.

ଓ ଓ

James 1:27: [27] Religion that God our Father accepts as pure and faultless is this: to look after orphans and widows in their distress and to keep oneself from being polluted by the world.

## Widows

Deuteronomy 26:12: [12] When you have finished setting aside a tenth of all your produce in the third year, the year of the tithe, you shall give it to the Levite, the alien, the fatherless and the widow, so that they may eat in your towns and be satisfied.

1 Timothy 5:3: [3] Give proper recognition to those widows who are really in need.

1 Timothy 5:16: [16] If any woman who is a believer has widows in her family, she should help them and not let the church be burdened with them, so that the church can help those widows who are really in need.

## Crippled

Matthew 15:30: [30] Great crowds came to him, bringing the lame, the blind, the crippled, the mute and many others, and laid them at his feet; and he healed them.

Luke 14:13-14: [13] "But when you give a banquet, invite the poor, the crippled, the lame, the blind, [14] and you will be blessed. Although they cannot repay you, you will be repaid at the resurrection of the righteous."

☙ ❧

Luke 14:21: [21] "The servant came back and reported this to his master. Then the owner of the house became angry and ordered his servant, 'Go out quickly into the streets and alleys of the town and bring in the poor, the crippled, the blind and the lame.'"

## Alien (Foreigner)

Deuteronomy 10:18: [18] He defends the cause of the fatherless and the widow, and loves the alien, giving him food and clothing.

☙ ❧

Deuteronomy 24:19: [19] When you are harvesting in your field and you overlook a sheaf, do not go back to get it. Leave it for the alien, the fatherless and the widow, so that the LORD your God may bless you in all the work of your hands.

☙ ❧

Psalm 146:9: [9] The LORD watches over the alien and sustains the fatherless and the widow, but he frustrates the ways of the wicked.

## Poor (and prisoners)

Deuteronomy 15:7: [7] If there is a poor man among your brothers in any of the towns of the land that the LORD your God is giving you, do not be hardhearted or tightfisted toward your poor brother.

☙ ❧

Proverbs 19:17: [17] He who is kind to the poor lends to the LORD, and he will reward him for what he has done.

Proverbs 28:27: [27] He who gives to the poor will lack nothing, but he who closes his eyes to them receives many curses.

Proverbs 29:7: [7] The righteous care about justice for the poor, but the wicked have no such concern.

**Multiple Facets of SNOWCAP in one passage**

Job 29:11-17: [11] "Whoever heard me spoke well of me,
and those who saw me commended me,
[12] because I rescued the poor who cried for help,
and the fatherless who had none to assist them.
[13] The one who was dying blessed me;
I made the widow's heart sing.
[14] I put on righteousness as my clothing;
justice was my robe and my turban.
[15] I was eyes to the blind
and feet to the lame.
[16] I was a father to the needy;
I took up the case of the stranger.
[17] I broke the fangs of the wicked
and snatched the victims from their teeth."

(See also Job 31:16-23.)

Isaiah 58:6-7: [6] "Is not this the kind of fasting I have chosen:
to loose the chains of injustice
and untie the cords of the yoke,
to set the oppressed free
and break every yoke?
[7] Is it not to share your food with the hungry
and to provide the poor wanderer with shelter—
when you see the naked, to clothe them,
and not to turn away from your own flesh and blood?"

Matthew 25:34-36: [34] "Then the King will say to those on his right, 'Come, you who are blessed by my Father; take your inheritance, the kingdom prepared for you since the creation of the world. [35] For I was hungry and you gave me something to eat, I was thirsty and you gave me something to drink, I was a stranger and you invited me in, [36] I needed clothes and you clothed me, I was sick and you looked after me, I was in prison and you came to visit me.'"

**Questions for Reflection**

Can you identify S.N.O.W.C.A.P. people in your neighborhood or community who need help?

Do any of these have a special place in your heart?

If so, why is that?

Was there a time in your life when you needed special help?

How did that experience change your perspective toward S.N.O.W.C.A.P. people?

From a standpoint of building God's kingdom, why are these strategic people to help?

What resources do you have available to help meet other's needs?

Are you willing to part with those resources?

Have you considered volunteering at an agency that serves S.N.O.W.C.A.P. people, or serving them on your own?

# Hospitality

**Wisdom from the Word**

Romans 12:13: [13] Share with the Lord's people who are in need. Practice hospitality.

ଓ ଓ

1 Timothy 5:9-10: [9] No widow may be put on the list of widows unless she is over sixty, has been faithful to her husband, [10] and is well known for her good deeds, such as bringing up children, showing hospitality, washing the feet of the Lord's people, helping those in trouble and devoting herself to all kinds of good deeds.

ଓ ଓ

Titus 1:7-8: [7] Since an overseer manages God's household, he must be blameless—not overbearing, not quick-tempered, not given to drunkenness, not violent, not pursuing dishonest gain. [8] Rather, he must be hospitable, one who loves what is good, who is self-controlled, upright, holy and disciplined.

ଓ ଓ

Hebrews 13:1-2: [1] Keep on loving one another as brothers and sisters. [2] Do not forget to show hospitality to strangers, for by so doing some people have shown hospitality to angels without knowing it.

ଓ ଓ

1 Peter 4:9: [9] Offer hospitality to one another without grumbling.

ଓ ଓ

## Questions for Reflection

At various times in history, Christians have been known for hospitality. Do you think this is typical of American Christians today?

Why or why not?

What concerns or fears do you have regarding opening your home for hospitality?

What safety guidelines would be wise to follow?

Is hospitality place-based or attitude-based?

What is the attitude behind hospitality?

What are some of the goals of hospitality?

If you already practice hospitality, what benefits have you noticed?

What are some other benefits of hospitality?

How do you, or could you, practice hospitality outside of your home?

# If "Money Talks," What Does it Say?

**Quotes from the Author**

MONEY says, "I'm not important. I'm not even real."

MONEY says, "I cannot provide security because I can be lost or stolen, and I am not a store of value because I have no intrinsic worth."

MONEY says, "I only work as a medium of exchange because the government requires everyone to accept me for payment of goods and services."

MONEY says, "The only things I'm good for are buying goods and services for myself or others."

## *Who Else is Thinking and Talking?*

**Quotes from the Author**

ARROGANCE thinks, "I deserve more than others."

HUMILITY thinks, "I deserve less than I have."

☙ ❧

INGRATITUDE says, "I should have more."

GRATITUDE says, "Thank you for _____, _____, _____ …"

☙ ❧

DISCONTENTMENT says, "I need more than I have to be happy"

CONTENTMENT says, "I need less than I have to be happy."

☙ ❧

ENVY says, "I want what they have."
COMPASSION says, "They need what I have."

☙ ❧

WORRY says, "I'm not sure how to get everything I need, and even if I do get everything I need, I might lose something."

SECURITY says, "Nothing that makes me truly rich can be taken away from me."

☙ ❧

TRUST thinks, "God knows everything I need, even before I do, and will provide each thing when the timing is perfect. If he takes something away, it's for my own good."

PRAYER says what trust thinks. It asks because it trusts (or because it's desperate).

☙ ❧

GREED asks, "How can I get even more, because I deserve it?"

GENEROSITY asks, "How can I give even more, because they need it?"

☙ ❧

SELFISH AMBITION asks, "How can I get more than them, even if I have to take it away?"

STEWARDSHIP asks, "How can I multiply my master's wealth to benefit more people?"

☙ ❧

# Generation Series

Experience the Generation Series through four business parables, encountering interesting characters who reveal practical insights about work, money, life dreams, love, and people. But be careful, the trajectory of your life might change in the process.

Book 1 – **Kids Work**

*The Benefits They Receive When Kids Work.* Meet James, who starts out torn between a gang and the law, and his neighbor, Ron Powers. Will James go to the juvenile center? Will he work with Ron? How will his decisions affect the direction of his life? This fast-moving story illustrates how enabling kids to work brings many benefits and prepares them for the real world.

Book 2 – **Dream House**

*Dream House Debt Free 8-12 Years From Now.* Eavesdrop as Ron Powers teaches his niece, Sofia, how she can acquire her dream house, and pay it off in 8-12 years. They bond over time as he shares many practical tips everyone could use to improve their personal finances, regardless of age or housing situation.

Book 3 – **Retire Successfully**

*Seven Key Areas Needed to Retire Successfully.* We got to know Sofia in Dream House. One of her workmates asks her how to prepare for a successful retirement and she is happy to share her secrets. Follow her example and you could be ready for your own successful retirement adventure.

Book 4 – **Legacy Living**

*Be Rich Through Legacy Living.* After Lydia is puzzled by a very disturbing dream, she turns to her cousin, Jackie, to help solve the mystery. In the process, Jackie introduces her to some unforgettable people, and Lydia will never be the same. You might not be either.

## Connect with the Author

*Would you like to connect with the author? Please feel free to reach out at:* **info@famfocfinancial.com**.

## About Family Focused Financial

Family Focused Financial specializes in retirement planning and services from a biblical mindset. Securities and Advisory Services are offered through ***Harbour Investments, Inc.*** Member FINRA/SIPC

FAMILY FOCUSED
FINANCIAL

*Scan Here!*

**Phone:** 269-208-4237
**Website:** www.famfocfinancial.com
**Email:** Info@famfocfinancial.com

Made in the USA
Monee, IL
04 November 2026

67379960R00075